The Inextinguishable Blaze

God's Call to Holiness, Repentance, Intimacy and Spiritual Awakening

By R. Maurice Smith

I0138707

RISING
RIVER
MEDIA

Published by Rising River Media, P. O. Box 9133, Spokane, Washington 99209

www.risingrivermedia.org

Cover design & original art work by Gale A. Smith.
Cover photo and inside art licensed through istock.

ISBN 13   978-0-9960096-6-9

Table of Contents

Reflections On Job, Repentance and Intimacy
(215)

If Only He Could Trust Us (225)

*"Fire shall be kept burning continually on the altar;
it is not to go out."*

(Leviticus 6:13)

Thou Who Camest From Above

THOU who camest from above
The pure celestial fire to impart,
Kindle a flame of sacred love
On the mean altar of my heart!
There let it for thy glory burn
With inextinguishable blaze;
And trembling to its source return,
In humble prayer and fervent praise.

Jesus, confirm my heart's desire
To work, and speak, and think for thee;
Still let me guard the holy fire,
And still stir up thy gift in me;
Ready for all thy perfect will,
My acts of faith and love repeat,
Till death thy endless mercies seal,
And make the sacrifice complete.

- Charles Wesley -
(Based upon Leviticus 6:13)

Author's Preface
To The Revised Edition

One of my favorite authors, Tom Clancy, once observed that war is simply *"theft writ large."* While it is a catchy - even brilliant - observation, it is also a generalization offered to make a valid point. In a similar vein of thought, I want to suggest that books like this one are also *"generalizations writ large."* That doesn't mean they aren't true or valid, but that they are designed and intended to communicate a message and to make a point. Whenever we use a broad brush - a generalization - in order to make a valid point, someone inevitably feels obligated to bring forward notable exceptions, as if the existence of exceptions invalidates the point being made. But an exception is exactly that - an exception to an otherwise pervasive situation. I thank God for exceptions. They remind us that even in the worst of times and conditions, God is still on the throne - alive and at work among His people. The book of Ruth, which begins with the words *"In the days when the judges ruled"* (Ruth 1:1), portrays God's faithfulness and the faithfulness of two women against the backdrop of the chaos, ugliness and unfaithfulness so prevalent during *"the days when the judges ruled."* The Book of Ruth is a beautiful exception to the generalization made four times by the author of the book of Judges, *"In those days there was no king in Israel. Everyone did what was right in his own eyes."* (Judges 17:6; 18:1; 19:1; 21:25) Generalizations speak truth, even in the face of notable exceptions. It is my prayer that whatever generalizations I make in the course of this book regarding the state of the contemporary Church will be understood in this light.

I have spent the past decade laboring in the organic house church movement, having spent the prior three decades in the traditional institutional Church. I love the Church - the betrothed bride of the Risen Christ - in all of its

The Inextinguishable Blaze

manifestations, but my heart remains in the organic church movement. I have written extensively over the past decade about what I believe God wants to do in and through the organic house church movement. But I have recently sensed the need to issue several words of admonishment to my house church friends. Upon reflection, many of the things I have said regarding the organic house church movement are also applicable to the Church at large in America, and for that reason I believe it is worth repeating some of those words here.

The organic house church movement as we know it today, and as I have experienced it over the past ten years, represents the best work of some of the brightest minds in the evangelical church. You simply cannot spend time around people like Wolfgang Simson, Neil Cole, John White or Tony and Felicity Dale (and many others I could name) without being impressed that God has raised up amazing leadership in the organic house church movement. They are people who share a genuine love for God and His Church. But at the end of the day, that's not enough.

In spite of excellent leadership, the organic house church movement has fallen victim to its own success. Multitudes of people responded to the promise of organic house church and went looking for what they had not found in more traditional expressions of Church. What many of those seekers discovered was that the advocates of organic house church had, in fact, *"over promised and under delivered."* We promised spiritual *Canaan* - the promised land of genuine New Testament Church and community, un-encumbered by traditional baggage. What too many hungry seekers found was smaller versions of what they had left. My friend John White refers to this phenomenon as *"Honey, I shrunk the church."* Simply stated, more often than not, we failed to deliver. In light of this failure to deliver, one of my ongoing

From The Author

fears has been that the organic house church movement would become co-opted by teachers who reduce it to a book writing, conference holding, note taking, notebook producing movement that seeks to offer *"Fire Building 101"* courses taught by people with no burns. And that brings us to this book.

Everything I have said about the organic house church movement is also true regarding the greater Church in America and the West. We both need something that only God can give. He has done it in the past, and He can do it again. But it cannot be obtained by means of any program, activity or act of self-effort. It is a sovereign act of God in response to and in fulfillment of the heart-cry found In Isaiah 64:1, *"Oh, that Thou wouldst rend the heavens and come down."* We need a divine visitation. The Church of God desperately needs a burning coal fresh from God's altar that turns smart Christians into flaming radicals - carriers of that "inextinguishable blaze" which, throughout the history of the Church, has set the world on fire for Christ. This book represents my meager effort to strike a match, which I pray will become a fire.

Finally, I want to take the opportunity of this Revised and Updated Edition to thank those readers of the original edition who have offered feed back and pointed needed corrections. Many thanks!

Maurice Smith
January, 2015

The Inextinguishable Blaze

Introduction

"John answered and said to them all, 'As for me, I baptize you with water; but One is coming who is mightier than I, and I am not fit to untie the thong of His sandals; He will baptize you with the Holy Spirit and fire.'" (Luke 3:16)

It is almost a principle of biblical interpretation that God's prophets frequently didn't fully understand the things they were prophesying. God spoke, so they spoke. And God took responsibility for its accuracy, its interpretation and its fulfillment. This prophecy from John the Baptist represents a case in point. Many (if not most) biblical commentators believe that John thought he was prophesying two different things - a baptism of the Holy Spirit in blessing, and a baptism of fire in judgement. It probably never occurred to John that the baptism of the Holy Spirit would, in fact, be a baptism of fire. Not the fire of God's judgment, but the fire of His Presence, His Power and His Holiness. And yet, that is precisely what happened on the Day of Pentecost.[1]

When God reached down with power from on high and touched those first believers gathered for prayer in the Upper Room on the Day of Pentecost, He didn't touch them with a new 40-day program for a more powerful Christian life, a new political strategy for electing better Emperors, a new prosperity scheme, or a new system of theology. He touched them with fire; the fire of the Holy Spirit, *"and divided tongues of fire appeared to them and rested upon each of them"* (Acts 2:3). He touched them with *"the Inextinguishable Blaze"* of His very Presence. That fire burned through the early Church

---

[1] I would suggest that John's prophecy actually has a double fulfillment. The first fulfillment took place on the day of Pentecost. The second fulfillment will - as I believe John understood - will take place at the End of the Age and on the day of judgment when God will judge all things by fire.

The Inextinguishable Blaze

for a generation (or more), empowering them to establish vibrant fellowships throughout the Roman world and to turn their world upside down in the Name of Jesus.[2]

This has been both the biblical and the historic pattern over the past 2000 years of Church history. Whenever the Church has fallen into disrepair, disrepute, and dysfunctionality, God has intervened with a fresh outpouring of the fire of His Spirit to renew His Church, to redeem the lost and to grow His Kingdom. To deny this reality is to deny the facts of God's gracious dealings with His people throughout history. A humorous example of this reality comes to us from the early years leading up to the Great Welsh Revival of 1904. At the turn of the 20th Century, as signs of a possible coming revival began to manifest in churches around America, one Presbyterian commentator observed, *"Theoretically, we are opposed to revivals and in favor of an even and uninterrupted growth of the Churches, but unfortunately, the facts are against us."*[3] That's refreshing honesty, because the facts were, and continue to be, against those who would minimize the role of spiritual awakenings and outpourings. Throughout Scripture and history, God's gracious visitations represent nothing less than the life-breath of the Church, bringing the Church of God to correction, repentance and

---

[2] The English Standard Version. The study note in the ESV Study Bible for this verse helps to make our point: *"The divided tongues of fire were not literal flames but looked enough like fire that this was the best description that could be given. "Fire" in the OT often indicates the presence of God, especially in his burning holiness and purity, consuming everything that is impure"*

[3] **Presbyterian Journal**, Philadelphia, cited in **Western Christian Advocate**, Indiana, September 19, 1900, quoted by Orr, **The Flaming Tongue**: *The Impact of Twentieth Century Revivals* (Chicago: Moody Press, 1973), page 67.

Introduction

fresh empowerment.

This is not simply another book about the need for greater "holiness" in the Church. There are excellent books available on that topic. This is a book about our desperate need for spiritual awakening. This is a book about our need to recover the fire of God's Presence among His people, a Presence that will ultimately

> *"The Church today in the opening decades of the 21st Century desperately needs a touch from God that will once again set His people and His Church ablaze with holy fire."*

manifest itself in three ways. *First*, it will manifest in an overwhelming sense of God's holiness and the genuine fear of God which accompanies it. By holiness I am not referring to any set of man-made rules for better behavior. The holiness I am referring to in this book is the holiness of God's Presence - that holiness which is nothing less than "a consuming fire" in the midst of God's people. *Second*, it will manifest in a powerful spirit of genuine personal repentance over sin among God's people, not the formalized "repentance" (or "pseudo-repentance") events which have become common in certain quarters of the Church over the past several years. God intends to bring about real repentance in the lives of real people for real sin. *Third*, it will manifest in a renewed and deepened sense of spiritual intimacy with God. This book is a call for believers to zealously pursue these three things in the firm belief that God will answer.

The Church today in the opening decades of the 21st Century desperately needs a touch from God that will once again set His people and His Church ablaze with holy fire. We need

The Inextinguishable Blaze

"the Inextinguishable Blaze" of God's Presence and holiness to once again become *"a fire in the minds of men."* This book is a call to zealously pursue the God of Holiness Who is a consuming fire, and, in the process, to once again think right thoughts about God, about our role in His Kingdom and about our calling and mission to a fallen world. God is indeed preparing His Church for a divine visitation of His Presence in a season of spiritual revival and awakening. The only question is whether or not you and I are willing to pursue it on His terms.

Are you?

"The church that can't worship must be entertained. And men who can't lead a church to worship must provide the entertainment." - A.W. Tozer.

"If the presence of God is in the church, the church will draw the world in. If the presence of God is not in the church, the world will draw the church out." - Charles Finney

"Religion today is not transforming people; rather it is being transformed by the people. It is not raising the moral level of society; it is descending to society's own level, and congratulating itself that it has scored a victory because society is smilingly accepting its surrender." - A. W. Tozer

"Lastly - are not the Church in their present state, a standing, public, perpetual denial of the gospel? Do they not stand out before the world, as a living, unanswerable contradiction of the gospel; and do more to harden sinners and lead them into a spirit of caviling and infidelity, than all the efforts of professed infidels from the beginning of the world to the present day?" - Charles Finney

"The nature of Christ's salvation is woefully misrepresented by the present-day evangelist. He announces a Saviour from Hell rather than a Saviour from sin. And that is why so many are fatally deceived, for there are multitudes who wish to escape the Lake of Fire who have no desire to be delivered from their carnality and worldliness." - A.W. Pink

The Inextinguishable Blaze

"Any objection to the carryings on of our present gold-calf Christianity is met with the triumphant reply, 'But we are winning them!' And winning them to what? To true discipleship? To cross-carrying? To self-denial? To separation from the world? To crucifixion of the flesh? To holy living? To nobility of character? To a despising of the world's treasures? To hard self-discipline? To love for God? To total committal to Christ? Of course the answer to all these questions is no." - A.W. Tozer

Chapter 1

A Fire In The Minds of Men

'The fire is in the minds of men, not in the roofs of buildings' - Dostoevsky

Some 30 years ago Dr. James H. Billington published a study of revolutionary movements in which he chronicled the *"origins of the revolutionary faith,"* including the nationalist and socialist revolutions of the 18th and 19th centuries (specifically the French and Russian revolutions). The metaphor of "fire," he argued, was an appropriate metaphor for the modern secular "revolutionary faith" because *"modern revolutionaries are believers, no less committed and intense than were the Christians or Muslims of an earlier era."* Billington went on to suggest that this revolutionary faith is *"perhaps the faith of our time."* [4]

It is important that you and I fully grasp what is being said here. Dr. Billington was asserting that a fundamental shift has taken place in the driving forces behind Western Culture and, by extension, the Church. You could fairly describe it as the shift from one religious view (biblical and Judeo-Christian) to another religious view (secular and humanist). Dr. Billington asserted that a new secular "faith in revolution" to effect social change has replaced the Christian "faith in revelation"

---

[4]James H. Billington, **Fire in the Minds of Men: Origins of the Revolutionary Faith** (New York: Basic Books, 1980), 677 pages. Dr. Billington adopted the phrase "fire in the minds of men" from Dostoevsky's work **The Possessed**, a fictional portrayal of the spread of revolutionary ideology. According to Billington, Dostoevsky *"depicted a stagnant (tranquil?) provincial town that was suddenly inspired (infected?) by new ideas. Shortly after a turbulent literary evening, a mysterious fire broke out; and a local official shouted out into the nocturnal confusion: 'The fire is in the minds of men, not in the roofs of buildings'"* (Billington, page 5)

The Inextinguishable Blaze

to effect social change through spiritual awakening and personal conversion. Revolution has replaced revelation. Secular faith in revolution, according to Dr. Billington, had become *"the faith of our time."*[5] Simply

". . . a fundamental shift has taken place in the driving forces behind Western Culture and, by extension, the Church."

put, the hope of our time, our people and our nation now lies in the "religion" of secular political revolution, the new *"fire in the minds of men,"* driving them to change the world through revolutionary political and social action. The "fire of men" has replaced the "fire of God." Revolution has replaced revelation. Social action has replaced spiritual awakening.

The Roots of Change

The roots of this radical shift had been growing without much fanfare for some time, but their growth accelerated and became much more public in the decades following World War 2. During my seminary days I was privileged to spend a summer term studying under the late Dr. Carl F. H. Henry, the founding editor of *Christianity Today* magazine and a brilliant Christian apologist. According to Dr. Henry, the 20th century witnessed the most radical reversal of ideas and ideals in human history. Dr. Henry observed that at the beginning of the 20th century textbooks referred to the God of the Bible, and the 10 commandments. There was an emphasis upon revealed values, upon the need for an internal change within man in order to achieve "Utopia." But by World War 2 something had happened. Following WW 2, references suddenly changed from the God of the Bible to

---

[5]Dr. Billington's use of the word "faith" to describe this new "revolutionary faith" makes it a "religious" view.

A Fire In The Minds Of Men

"Nature's God" or "God" in general. Rather than revealed values, the new emphasis was upon shared values. And rather than a change needed in man, the emphasis was placed upon change through education.

> *"Revolution has replaced revelation. Social action has replaced spiritual awakening."*

Finally, in the last half of the 20th century all theistic aspects and references to God had been eliminated. God now counted for nothing in education or in public life. Instead of shared values, the emphasis of the late 20th century was upon the tolerance of diverse values. Instead of change by education and legislation, the emphasis was upon change through revolution and violence. In other words, a radical shift was underway, a shift away from biblical faith, revelation and spiritual awakening, and toward a secular faith in revolution and violence to effect change.

This philosophical earthquake found theological expression in the writings of the French existentialist and theologian from Syracuse, Dr. Gabriel Vahanian, who summarized it well in his book, *The Death of God: The Culture of our Post-Christian Era.* Summarizing the thinking of many Post-WW2 philosophers and theologians, Vahanian wrote, *"The fundamentals of modern culture are neither non-Christian nor anti-Christian; they are post-Christian. They are derived from Christianity, yet in them Christianity suffers 'not a torture death but a quiet euthanasia.' It may be that our age still is religious. But it is certainly post-Christian."* [6]

In his Introduction to Vahanian's book, Dr. Paul Ramsey, a Professor of Religion and Christian ethicist at Princeton

---

[6]Gabriel Vahanian, *The Death of God: The Culture of our Post Christian Era* (New York: George Braziller, 1961) p. xxxiii.

The Inextinguishable Blaze

University, made two observations which are important for our discussion. First, he suggested that *"every revival of Christianity in the past three hundred years has revived less of it, and each was less and less an enduring revival."* In other words, Dr. Ramsey was declaring that faith in "revival" or spiritual awakening is no longer a viable option or hope for our future. Second, he observed that, *"Ours is the first attempt in recorded history to build a culture upon the premise that God is dead.* Dr. Ramsey went on to say, *"The period post mortem Dei divides into two distinct eras, roughly at some point between the World Wars. Until that time, the cultural death of God meant something anti-Christian; after it and until now, the death of God means something entirely post-Christian."*

For his part, Dr. Vahanian emphasized three essential points. He argued that ours is a post-Christian world where (1) *"Christianity has sunk into religiosity,"* (2) *"modern culture is gradually losing the marks of that Christianity which brought it into being and shaped it,"* and (3) *"tolerance has become religious syncretism."* It's sort of hard to argue against those observations, isn't it?!

In a subsequent work Dr. Vahanian explained further, *"This does not mean, obviously, that God Himself no longer is but that, regardless of whether he is or not, his reality, as the Christian tradition has presented it, has become culturally irrelevant: God is de trop, as Sarte would say."* [7] If God is truly "dead" (i.e., irrelevant for any practical purposes), then

---

[7]"de trop," French for "too much, unnecessary, superfluous." Gabriel Vahanian, *Wait Without Idols* (New York: George Braziller, 1964) p. 31-32. For an excellent treatment of the "death of God" movement from a biblical perspective and its implications for the Church see John Warwick Montgomery, *The Suicide of Christian Theology* (Minneapolis: Bethany Fellowship, 1970).

A Fire In The Minds Of Men

so is any "faith in revelation" vision for spiritual awakening and transformation that depends upon God's existence.

A Church Caught Between Two Competing Visions

This is the "new reality" in which the post-World War 2 Postmodern Evangelical Church in America and the West now finds itself - a Church which by most measurements today is more politically correct than biblically correct. The Church of the early 21st Century finds itself confronted and challenged by two competing and opposite visions of reality and the future. And it quickly becomes clear to the historian of religion and philosophy that the vision which Dr. Billington portrayed as the rise of a "faith in Revolution" was built solidly upon the conclusions of men like Ramsey and Vahanian, because they, too, had rejected revelation in favor of revolution. Billington was simply arguing and announcing a conclusion for which others had already paved the way. In doing so he outlined the basic challenge for the Church in our time, the challenge between two competing visions of the future.

On the one hand we are confronted with a secular faith and vision of change through political action and revolution. On the other hand we are confronted with a biblical faith and vision of change through spiritual awakening. And the conflict between these two competing visions helps to explain the behavior of the Evangelical Church over the past 30 years.

> *"The Church of the early 21st Century finds itself confronted and challenged by two competing and opposite visions of reality and the future."*

When Dr. Billington suggested that this revolutionary faith is

The Inextinguishable Blaze

"perhaps the faith of our time" he was more correct than we would like to admit. I would argue that this secular faith in revolution to effect political change has now been adopted by the Evangelical Church. In the thinking of many of God's people today, faith in political revolution has replaced faith in revelation and spiritual awakening. And that statement demands an explanation.

In the thirty-plus years since 1980 and the election of Ronald Reagan (to focus on recent history, although we could go back further) Evangelical Christians have become increasingly involved in "political revolution" through such movements as the rise of the Christian Coalition, the Moral Majority, the Tea Party and any number of other activities which have collectively become known as the "Christian right" or the "religious right" or the "conservative right." The "operating thesis" behind all such conservative Christian political movements has been that by our active participation in the process of political revolution we could transform society along biblical lines, and, perhaps, even usher in a spiritual awakening.

But after thirty-plus years of actively pursuing "political revolution no one can say with a straight face that America is more biblical or more Christian than it was in 1980. Indeed, the situation was summed up very concisely over ten years ago by Paul Weyrich, the intellectual father of the Moral Majority, and an acknowledged founding father of the "conservative religious right." [8] In February of 1999, shortly after the United States Senate failed to convict and impeach

---

[8]The September 6, 1999 issue of *Christianity Today* magazine reprinted Mr. Weyrich's letter, along with responses by six leading evangelicals, including Ralph Reed, Cal Thomas, Jerry Falwell, Don Eberly (his response is particularly good), James Dobson and Charles Colson. These are a must read.

A Fire In The Minds Of Men

President Bill Clinton for his behavior in the Monica Lewinski affair, Weyrich sent an open letter to his constituents announcing that, in his opinion, cultural conservatives (including Evangelical Christians) had lost their "cultural war of attrition" which he had helped launch some twenty years earlier:

"In looking at the long history of conservative politics, from the defeat of Robert Taft in 1952, to the nomination of Barry Goldwater, to the takeover of the Republican Party in 1994, I think it is fair to say that conservatives have learned to succeed in politics. That is, we got our people elected. But that did not result in the adoption of our agenda. The reason, I think, is that politics itself has failed. And politics has failed because of the collapse of the culture. The culture we are living in becomes an ever-wider sewer. In truth, I think we are caught up in a cultural collapse of historic proportions, a collapse so great that it simply overwhelms politics."

Simply put, the Church's adoption of the "faith in revolution" movement had failed to yield the anticipated - even promised - fruit of a more biblical or Christian society, not to mention the absence of any "spiritual awakening." Why? Because we had reversed the process in the false hope that by adopting the "faith" of the Enemy we could achieve the purpose and results of God (a spiritually transformed society). We had failed to learn and understand the lesson of church history, namely, that the fires of "faith in revelation" expressed through revival and spiritual awakening have frequently transformed the society of which they are a part. But the secular fires of "faith in revolution" have never yielded spiritual awakening or a society transformed along biblical lines.

The Inextinguishable Blaze

What 30 years of conservative Christian political "revolution" had yielded was a noticeable rise among Christians and other conservatives of "conspiracy" theories for why our efforts at political

"The adoption of a false vision and a false faith inevitably leads to false explanations for its failure."

revolution had failed. It was the fault of secret power brokers such as the Illuminati, the Tri-Lateral Commission, the Bildebergers, the proponents of a New World Order, the United Nations and a host of other shadowy individuals and organizations who secretly manipulated the true levers of power. The adoption of a false vision and a false faith inevitably leads to false explanations for its failure. "False fire" always burns in the wrong direction. In the process, Evangelical Christians had failed to heed the warning of God to the Prophet Isaiah regarding the power conspiracies of his own days:

"For thus the LORD spoke to me with mighty power and instructed me not to walk in the way of this people, saying, "You are not to say, 'It is a conspiracy!' In regard to all that this people call a conspiracy, And you are not to fear what they fear or be in dread of it. It is the LORD of hosts whom you should regard as holy. And He shall be your fear, And He shall be your dread." (Isaiah 8:11-13)

Do you hear what God was saying to Isaiah? He is still saying the same thing to the conspiracy advocates of today. His message is simple and clear. He who fears God fears no man or any man-made conspiracy, whether real or imaginary (see Psalm 2). The secular fires of political revolution represent nothing less than the spiritual counterfeit of the Enemy of mankind, designed and intended to distract men

A Fire In The Minds Of Men

from the truth by convincing them that their salvation rests on political revolution and self-improvement, rather than resting on God's revelation, spiritual awakening and spiritual re-birth.

Lessons From History

Historically speaking, these two competing visions have yielded strikingly different results in the lives of men and nations. And history is not kind to the proponents of this "faith in revolution." Indeed, those who have placed their faith in the "fools gold" of revolution have always paid a high price for their faith. A few examples (among many that could be cited) will help make the point. The French revolution, a movement frequently regarded as the model and archetype of the "faith in revolution" movement, produced an estimated death toll between a low of 1million to a high of 3 million. But the "faith in revolution" delusion was just getting warmed up. The Communist Revolution of Jozef Stalin (USSR, 1932-39) killed an estimated 23 million through its many "purges" of the "unfaithful," including the inhumanely brutal Great Ukrainian Famine. But the "faith in revolution" movement had not yet reached its zenith. That honor (or horror) awaited the arrival of Mao Ze-Dong ("Chairman Mao") and his revolution in China (1958-69). In that one revolution alone the fires of the "faith in revolution" movement sacrificed an estimated 49-to-78 million victims on its altar of revolution. In a sad exclamation point to the abysmal history of the "faith in revolution" movement, former U.S. Secretary of Defense Robert McNamara once observed that by his estimation all the wars of the 20th Century (most of which had their roots in the "faith in revolution" movement) had claimed the lives of some 170 million people. Welcome to the bloody altar of human sacrifice at the heart of the "faith in revolution" religion.

Standing in stark contrast to the history of the "faith in

The Inextinguishable Blaze

revolution" movement is its opposite: those spiritual fires in the hearts of men which have historically found expression in those "faith in revelation" movements we refer to as spiritual awakening and revival. Collectively speaking, the fires of revelation and spiritual awakening have produced far greater good than all the fires of secular revolution of the past 200 years combined. While France was suffering under the delusions of "faith in revolution" during the French Revolution, England was experiencing the blessings of the Evangelical Awakening, led by such men as George Whitefield, John and Charles Wesley and many others. Beginning in roughly 1740, the fires of the Evangelical Awakening in England initiated a 100 year period of profound social transformation throughout England which saw the establishment of child labor laws for the protection of children in the workplace, the establishment of "Sunday Schools" for their education (Sunday was the only day they didn't work and could go to school), the peaceful abolishment of slavery throughout England and its colonies and much more. [9]

Similar stories could be told about the Second Great Awakening on the American Frontier (1795-1811) and how it tamed the frontier, pulled it back from the abyss of anarchy and lawlessness, transformed the American Southeast into "the Bible Belt," [10] conquered Yale University and quenched the fires of French radicalism in America. We could give historic accounts of the Second Evangelical Awakening in England and how it further transformed English society, giving rise to The Salvation Army and tireless efforts by

---

[9] For more, see John Wesley Bready, *England Before And After Wesley* (New York: Stoughton & Stoughton, 1938).

[10] John B. Boles, *The Great Revival: Beginnings of the Bible Belt* (Lexington: The University of Kentucky Press, 1996, 1972)

A Fire In The Minds Of Men

Christians against such rampant social evils as poverty and child prostitution. And all of those historic accounts would simply reinforce the point we made earlier, namely, that the fires of revelation and spiritual awakening have produced far greater good than all the fires of secular revolution of the past 200 years combined.

". . . the fires of revelation and spiritual awakening have produced far greater good than all the fires of secular revolution of the past 200 years combined."

Who Owns The Future?

"As spring-time precedes summer, and seed-time harvest, so every great onward step in the social and political progress of Great Britain has ever been preceded by a national Revival of Religion. The sequence is as unmistakable as it is inevitable . . . . Hence it is not necessary to be Evangelical, Christian, or even religious, to regard with keen interest every stirring of popular enthusiasm that takes the familiar form of a Revival. Men may despise it, hate it, or fear it, but there is no mistaking its significance. It is the precursor of progress, the herald of advance. It may be as evanescent as the blossom of the orchard, but without it there would be no fruit." [11]

William Thomas Stead is known throughout schools of journalism around the world as the father of modern investigative journalism. Born in England in 1849, W. T. Stead was the son of a Congregational minister. Home-

---

[11] William Thomas Stead, *The Revival In The West* (London: The Review of Reviews, 1905), page 33.

The Inextinguishable Blaze

schooled by his father, by the age of five he could read both Latin and English. In 1861 Stead was sent to finish his education at a school for boys. While there he had a personal encounter with God, and was deeply touched. His life was set ablaze by the fires of the Second Evangelical Awakening, which had begun in Wales in 1859 and was then sweeping the country.

Rather than following his father into the ministry, the younger Stead chose a career in journalism. He would become perhaps the most renown journalist of 19th Century England. In his latter years he also become the chronicler of the fires of revival. When the

"Does our future and our hope in this world lie with God's 'revelation' or with the secular 'revolution' of men?

fires of revival broke out in South Wales in 1904 Stead traveled to South Wales, attended meetings and interviewed participants. His articles for denominational magazines as well as for his own publication *("The Review of Reviews")* helped to explain and popularize the revival for audiences in London and throughout England. In the context of reflecting on the role of spiritual awakenings in the history of Great Britain, and the "fires of revelation" which ignite such awakenings, Stead made the observation which I have quoted above. The question is, was he right?[12]

In the opening decades of the 21st Century the Evangelical Church in America and the West is confronted with a profound question: *"Who owns the future, and where does*

---

[12]For more on the life and work of W. T. Stead, see Chapter 10 in our book, *The Least of These: The Role of Good Deeds In A Jesus-Shaped Spirituality*, available on our website from Amazon.com.

A Fire In The Minds Of Men

our hope lie?" Does our future and our hope in this world lie with God's "revelation" or with the secular "revolution" of men? Our secular Postmodern Western Culture has concluded that the future of our world lies in the unproven hope that the fires of political revolution will bring about social change and a better life for all. Unfortunately for the prophets of secular revolution, as we have already pointed out, the track record of secular revolution is questionable on a good day, and disastrous on all other days. The clear teaching of Scripture and the historic experience of the Church combine to tell us that - apart from the return of Christ to establish His Kingdom - our future lies with the fires of revelation and spiritual awakening. These are the two choices which currently lie before us. There is no third choice. Unfortunately, too many professing Evangelical Christians today are placing their hope for the future in the fires of secular political and social revolution, rather than in the fires of spiritual revelation and spiritual awakening.

The Inextinguishable Blaze

It is time for God's church to reject and abandon the "fool's gold" and false fire of the "faith in revolution" movement and to once again recover *"the Inextinguishable Blaze"* - the fire of God's Presence in the life of His People. I believe it is the heart and the plan of God to restore our faith in His revelation of Himself by visiting His Church with the fresh fire of His Presence and holiness. He desires to once again set the hearts of His people ablaze with holy fire and to ignite a genuine spiritual awakening in our generation.

Consider this your personal call to embrace *"the Inextinguishable Blaze."*

The Inextinguishable Blaze

Chapter 2

What The Church Thinks About God

"What comes into our minds when we think about God is the most important thing about us." - A. W. Tozer

The secular "faith in revolution" movement could not have exploded on the cultural scene at a worse time in the life of the Evangelical Church. It came at time when the Church was losing its grip on its own role in society as well as its grip on who God is (remember the "death of God" movement we mentioned in the prior chapter?). The long-term impact of the cultural shift from "faith in revelation" to "faith in revolution" has been nothing short of devastating for the Church. It has largely succeeded in convincing our Postmodern culture that the organized Evangelical Church is irrelevant for all practical purposes. After all, according to the "faith in revolution" movement, political or social change can only come about by direct (and increasingly violent) revolution. Any Church, Christian organization or individual Christian who disagrees with this revolutionary paradigm is quickly written off as irrelevant (at best) or obstructionist (or worse, such as "bigoted"). The practical effect has been to ostracize and isolate the Church from the predominant cultural discussion regarding how to best change politics and society. But the "faith in revolution" movement could never have succeeded if it had not caught the Church in the midst of its own crisis over what it believes about God. And that is where we now want to turn attention.

> *". . . the 'faith in revolution' movement could never have succeeded if it had not caught the Church in the midst of its own crisis over what it believes about God."*

The Inextinguishable Blaze

In his classic book, ***The Knowledge of the Holy*** A. W. Tozer devotes the first chapter to a lengthy discussion concerning the importance of Christians thinking right thoughts about God. It is a chapter well worth making the effort to read. *"What comes into our minds when we think about God is the most important thing about us,"* declares Tozer.[13] He goes on to observe,

"A right conception of God is basic not only to systematic theology but to practical Christian living as well. It is to worship what the foundation is to the temple; where it is inadequate or out of plumb the whole structure must sooner or later collapse . . . . Before the Christian Church goes into eclipse anywhere there must first be a corrupting of her simple basic theology. She simply gets a wrong answer to the question, 'What is God like?" and goes on from there.'"[14]

The "Secret Law of the Soul"

Tozer's observations are breathtakingly profound, even today, a generation after they were first made. And perhaps no observation is more profound than this one:

"We tend by a secret law of the soul to move toward our mental image of God." [15]

This observation alone explains much of the current condition of the Church in the early decades of the 21st Century. The

---

[13]A. W. Tozer, ***The Knowledge of the Holy*** (Harper & Row: New York, 1961), page 9

[14]Ibid., page 10.

[15]Ibid,, page 9.

What The Church Thinks About God

Church is in serious trouble, and our low view of God is to blame. As Tozer adroitly observed, *"Low views of God destroy the gospel for all who hold them."* And low views of God abound in the modern Church. In the generation since Tozer commented on the condition of the Church, *"Therapy has usurped theology. Right thoughts about God have been replaced with good feelings about God and ourselves."* right thinking about God among Christians has given way to low views of God which, in prior generations of believers, would have constituted a scandal. Our nominal doctrinal statements remain orthodox. Our Systematic Theologies are plentiful and readily available. But neither our doctrinal statements nor our theologies hold any attraction for the mass of professing believers and church-goers. Therapy has usurped theology. Right thoughts about God have been replaced with good feelings about God and ourselves. And Scripture has been reduced to a "self-help" guide for people seeking personal fulfillment, a better marriage, more obedient children, a more prosperous financial future or simply seeking their "best life now."

Dr. Howard Hendricks once observed that we suffer from "the peril of the pendulum" - the tendency to swing from one extreme to the other. Professing Christians are no exception to this unwritten rule of human behavior. In the years since the Second World War, contemporary Western Christianity has witnessed a slow but massive swing of the theological pendulum. It has swung away from a faith and a theology which are "theo-centric" (God-Centered) and toward a faith and theology which are "anthropo-centric" (man-centered). The result has been a Postmodern view of God that prior generations of evangelical believers would never have recognized as biblical.

The Inextinguishable Blaze

Author Robert Peterson describes the situation well when he says, *"Here is the problem in a nutshell: Moderns will only accept a god who will meet them on their terms."*[16] And the terms of the modern Evangelical Church are simple: health,

"While the butler humbly accepts the praise we offer for a job well done, both parties understand who is really in charge here. After all, we can always hire a new butler."

wealth, success, political clout, along with assorted other blessings, delivered upon request. We pray, we proclaim and God obeys. And in the process, the Servant-King of Scripture, Who both rules His fallen creation and redeems His rebellious creatures has been reduced to a proper English butler who knows his place, takes instructions without murmuring, responds to our adulteries with an understanding, *"Will that be two for breakfast, sir?"* and always serves meals and treats on schedule as agreed. While the butler humbly accepts the praise we offer for a job well done, both parties understand who is really in charge here. After all, we can always hire a new butler. Such an idolatrous understanding of God, in addition to being unbiblical, is spiritually impotent to withstand the gale force winds of our Postmodern culture's "faith in revolution" movement, winds which are now coming against the Church with devastating results.

Idolatry And Lost Fire

"Among the sins to which the human heart is prone, hardly

---

[16]Robert Peterson, **Hell On Trial: The Case For Eternal Punishment**, P & R Publishing, P.O. Box 817, Phillipsburg, New Jersey, page 136

What The Church Thinks About God

any other is more hateful to God than idolatry, for idolatry is at bottom a libel on His character. The idolatrous heart assumes that God is other than He is - in itself a monstrous sin - and substitutes for the true God one made after its own likeness."[17]

Tozer's *"secret law of the soul"* has wreaked havoc in the contemporary Evangelical Church, whose poor spiritual condition is directly traceable to its diminished view of God and its exalted view of itself. Our diminished view of God has produced a generation of "Christian idolaters" - nominal professors and worshipers who *"simply imagine things about God and then act as if they were true."* [18]

We do not have the time or space in this small book to address all of the low views of God and the various "idolatries" of the present day Church which contribute to its low view of God. Rather, I want to focus our attention on one in particular. Of all the things the contemporary Church has lost as a consequence of its idolatry, perhaps the most devastating has been our loss of holiness. More specifically, we have lost our sense of God's holiness, our sense of our God as *"a consuming fire."*

To focus upon any one of God's attributes (those aspects of His essential nature) to the exclusion of others is to paint a distorted view of God as He relates to His people. In other words, we run the risk of practicing a subtle idolatry that imagines and portrays God other than He is. But the same is true if we exclude a particular attribute of God. And in the Postmodern Church of the early 21st Century the God we

---

[17]Tozer, **The Knowledge of the Holy**, page 11.

[18]Ibid., page 12.

The Inextinguishable Blaze

have created is no longer the God Whose holiness is "a consuming fire."

The Scriptures refer to God as "a consuming fire" no less than nine times.[19] Perhaps the most well known declaration of this truth is found at the end of Hebrews where the writer (quoting Deuteronomy 4:24) declares, *"Therefore, since we receive a kingdom which cannot be shaken, let us show gratitude, by which we may offer to God an acceptable service with reverence and awe; for our God is a consuming fire"* (Hebrews 12:28-29).

To understand the very Presence of God as a "consuming fire" is to understand something of His essential nature. The Psalmist understood this reality of God's Presence when he wrote under the inspiration of the Holy Spirit, *"The mountains melted like wax at the presence of the LORD, At the presence of the Lord of the whole earth"* (Psalm 97:5; see also Micah 1:4). For this reason alone it should come to us as no surprise that seasons of divine visitation, both in Scripture and in the historic experience of the Church, are frequently described in terms of "fire." Listen to the Prophet Isaiah as he openly longs for God's visitation, in Isaiah 64:1-2,

Oh, that Thou wouldst rend the heavens and come down,
That the mountains might quake at Thy presence
— As fire kindles the brushwood,
as fire causes water to boil —
To make Thy name known to Thine adversaries,
That the nations may tremble at Thy presence.

---

[19]Exodus 24:17; Deuteronomy 4:24; 9:3; Isaiah 29:6; 30:27 & 30; 33:14; Lamentations 2:3; Hebrews 12:29.

What The Church Thinks About God

Isaiah understood that the Presence of God is a fire that *"kindles the brushwood."* Isaiah was well acquainted with the fire of God's Presence. Early in his own ministry Isaiah himself had stood in God's Presence, had heard the Seraphim of heaven cry, *"Holy, Holy, Holy, is the LORD of hosts, The whole earth is full of His glory,"* and had been touched by burning coals fresh from God's altar (Isaiah 6:1-6). As a result of that experience Isaiah understood that when God's Presence comes, it comes like "a consuming fire" that burns and consumes whatever is unholy, and produces holiness in the lives of those it touches. He is holy.

"We've Been Robbed!"

When the Evangelical Church gave up its "faith in revelation" in the years following World War 2 and embraced our Postmodern culture's "faith in revolution," the Church found itself robbed of three things which it could not afford to lose.

First, the Church Has Been Robbed of Its Fire. The Evangelical Church has been robbed of any genuine sense of the Presence of God as "a consuming fire" of God's holiness along with the "fear of God" it produces in the lives of God's people. We have been robbed of that fire which has motivated and empowered the Church from the Day of Pentecost until now.

Second, the Church Has Been Robbed of the Fire of Genuine Personal Repentance. Whenever God visits His Church, the consuming fire of His Presence and holiness produces genuine personal and corporate repentance. We can see this clearly in the visitation of the Risen Christ to the Seven Churches of Asia in Revelation Chapters 2-3. Next to the command to "listen," the most frequent command to the Churches of Revelation is "repent."

The Inextinguishable Blaze

Third, the Church Has Been Robbed of the Intimacy Which God Himself Desires. When the Evangelical Church lost its sense of God's holiness and fear, and the need for personal repentance from sin, it also lost the fire of genuine intimacy with God. Much of our supposed intimacy is little more than a mushy sentimentality that costs nothing and produces even less.

Ideas have consequences. And so does their loss. The present day loss of any genuine sense of God's Presence as "a consuming fire" along with the holiness and the biblical fear which accompany it, has produced consequences in the life of God's people which are nothing short of catastrophic. The love of God has been distorted into little more than grand-fatherly sentimentality. The holiness, fear and wrath of God have been excluded from our vocabulary. Repentance has been forgotten while sin has been either ignored or sanctified. The judgments of God have been muted and the Cross of Christ has been reduced to religious jewelry. Not only does this emasculated God want you to have your best life now, He now promises that when you die, regardless of your condition, you will eventually end up in heaven, a somewhat confused citizen of a Kingdom whose motto is *"holy to the Lord"* (Zechariah 14:20). Richard Neibuhr's classic observation regarding American Christianity, made over a generation ago, remains as one of the best summaries of the situation:

"A God without wrath brought men without sin into a kingdom without judgment through the ministrations of a Christ without a cross." [20]

---

[20]H. Richard Niebuhr, ***The Kingdom of God In America***, (New York, Willett, 1937), p. 193.

What The Church Thinks About God

Where's The Revival We Ordered?

Our diminished view of God and the idolatries we have embraced have affected our approach to the issue of revival and spiritual renewal. The Church today talks about and prays for revival as a time when God - in true English butler fashion - will

"Ideas have consequences. And so does their loss."

serve our agendas, fix our problems, bless what we are presently doing and give all our programs an upgrade. Gone is any notion that God might visit us, interrupt our programs, melt the "mountains" of our religious empires, confront our sins and quash our political revolutions. No. The god of our idolatry is little more than a divine fix-it man called in to fix what's broken while leaving as little "mess" behind as possible when He is done. And our "formula" for bringing about this blessing is as ignoble as our thoughts about God. We announce a 40-day season of fasting and prayer which will culminate on schedule with a celebration worship service where God will fulfill His obligation to make an appearance and bless the attendees, thereby enabling the Church staff to declare blessing, victory and revival - all while live streaming on the internet and selling large quantities of overpriced DVDs of the proceedings.

So, why doesn't God obey our formula for revival? Could it be that at its very core stands an idol fashioned by our own vain imaginations about God? Could it be possible that the Church has gotten a wrong answer to the question, *"What is God*

"The god of our idolatry is little more than a divine fix-it man called in to fix what's broken while leaving as little 'mess' behind as possible when He is done."

like," and has simply gone on from there? The absence of revival in our generation may well be attributable to three things: 1) our adoption of the secular "faith in revolution" view of reality, 2) our own idolatries and low view of God, and 3) our unwillingness to repent and seek Him on His terms, including holiness and repentance.

The Inextinguishable Blaze

It is time for the Church to once again think right thoughts about God. It is time for the Church to abandon our recent idolatries and to recover the God of Scripture in all of His power and holiness. We need a generation of believers who have recovered their vision for who God is and for what He wants to accomplish in this generation. We need a generation of believers willing to have their lives set on fire by God's Presence and holiness. God is calling His people to once again become bearers of *"the Inextinguishable Blaze."*

Are you prepared to answer the call?

Chapter 3

Children Of The Burning Heart

"To have found God and still pursue Him is the soul's paradox of love, scorned indeed by the too-easily-satisfied religionist, but justified in happy experience by the children of the burning heart . . . . Come near to the holy men and women of the past and you will soon feel the heat of their desire after God. They mourned for Him, they prayed and wrestled and sought for Him day and night, in season and out, and when they had found Him the finding was all the sweeter for the long seeking." [21]

By now, no warning should be necessary and the intent of this book should be clear. But I will offer a warning, anyway. Just to be fair. Be warned! This is a book with an agenda. I am a "spiritual arsonist"! My agenda is simple. I am looking for *"children of the burning heart,"* bearers of *"the inextinguishable blaze."* I am looking for believers whose hearts burn with the spiritual fires of revelation, revival and spiritual awakening. Should you be one of those unique individuals, what follows will ring true and you may even be tempted to pause, build and altar and worship. It happens. More often than most are aware. If, on the other hand, you are not one of these people, my goal - in the words of Charles Wesley - is to *"Kindle a flame of sacred love On the mean altar of (your) heart."* I want to ignite a divine fire and turn you into one of the *"children of the burning heart."* Don't take this lightly. The future of the Church, indeed, of our nation and our world depends upon your response.

---

[21]A.W. Tozer, **The Pursuit of God** (Harrisburg, PA: Christian Publications, 1948), Page 12.

The Inextinguishable Blaze

The Altar, The Sacrifice and The Fire

*"The altar is prepared,
the sacrifice is laid;
now, let the fire fall."*[22]

Children of the burning heart - bearers of *"the Inextinguishable Blaze"* - are not new. They litter the landscape of the Church like marker beacons which call travelers to remember *"the ancient paths, where the good way is, and walk in it Jeremiah"* (6:16). You will find such souls whenever you study the history of spiritual awakenings in the Church.

When I wrote my book on the great Welsh Revival of 1904 I discovered such a person in the Revival's best known leader - Evan Roberts. At the time the revival broke out under his ministry in the fall of 1904, Roberts was a 26 year old former coal miner who had just begun his first year of bible school in preparation for ministry. He later confided that he had been praying for revival for over ten years. According to those close to him, Roberts spent hours in solitary communion with God. One evening prior to the Revival while he was still in school, Roberts spent considerable time walking in the school garden in communion with God. He returned to his room around midnight, his face shining to the point of glowing. His roommate, Sidney Evans was astonished and asked, *"Evan, what has happened to you?"* *"Oh, Syd,"* he replied, *"I had a vision of all Wales being lifted up to heaven. We are going to see the mightiest revival that Wales has ever known - and the Holy Spirit is coming soon, so we must get ready."* Like Isaiah, and so many saints before him, Evan

---

[22]Evan Roberts in a letter on the eve of the Great Welsh Revival of 1904.

46

Children Of The Burning Heart

Roberts had stood in God's Presence and His heart had been set on fire by *"the Inextinguishable Blaze."*

Another burning heart I discovered in my study of the Welsh Revival was an evangelist by the name of Seth Joshua. Years after the revival his son, Dr. Peter Joshua (a retired Presbyterian pastor when he related this story) told about missing school one day and going to a local park to play. Suddenly he spotted his father walking in the park. Hiding in some bushes he watched as his father walked by:

"As he came near I was frightened as I heard that he was crying (something I thought never my Dad would ever do) and as he went by he was saying, 'Please God, give me Wales', and kept saying this as long as I could hear him. After a while I ran back home, and while I had to explain to mother that I had mitched school, I asked her what was wrong with Dad, and told her that I had heard him crying and saying 'Give me Wales.' She ruffled her hair and said, 'You'll understand one day.' God never gave Wales to my Dad, although he gave him many souls, but one day when he was preaching when he made an appeal Evan Roberts was the only one who stood to his feet and trusted the Saviour. God never gave Wales to my Dad, but he gave Wales to Evan Roberts."[23]

These, and many others of like company, are the *"children of the burning heart,"* bearers of *"the inextinguishable blaze."* Seeking God's Presence is their heart's desire, holiness and the fear of God is the beauty of their spiritual lives, genuine

---

[23] This anecdote is related in a letter in the possession of Mr. Meurig Thomas of Llangeler, Dyfed. A copy is in the Evangelical Library of Wales at Bridgend, quoted by Brynmor P. Jones, *Voices From The Welsh Revival 1904-1905* (Evangelical Press of Wales: Bridgend, 1995), page 16.

The Inextinguishable Blaze

personal repentance is a daily experience and they enjoy an intimacy with God that beggars description. Are you one of them?

By now it should be clear that the purpose of this book is as much incendiary as it is educational. This is by choice, not by accident. We are a Church besotted with teachers. Our seminaries (like the excellent one I attended oh so many years ago) turn them out by the bus load. It was not so much different a150 years ago in Charles

"You can no more teach your way into the fire of God's Presence than you can teach your way into a passionate marriage. Teaching is about technique. Fire and passion are something else entirely."

Haddon Spurgeon's day. When asked by one of his students at Spurgeon's College for the secret his preaching he replied, *"I am on fire for Christ. And when I preach, people come to watch me burn."* Spurgeon understood something we have forgotten. Knowledge and competency are not enough. We have raised up a generation of highly educated and immensely competent teachers, administrators, promoters, managers, fund raisers and media personalities (and even a few pastors) who can manage complex religious organizations. But where are the believers whose clothes carry the unmistakable smell of heavenly fire and whose lives are kindling for *"the Inextinguishable Blaze."* You can no more teach your way into the fire of God's Presence than you can teach your way into a passionate marriage. Teaching is about technique. Fire and passion are something else entirely.

So, again, consider yourself duly warned. I am a spiritual arsonist, you are the fuel, the fire comes fresh from God's

Children Of The Burning Heart

own altar. And, oh yes, there is no safe way to read this book.

"Fire On Ice"

"Will the Revival in South Wales be like a bonfire on ice ? Or will it set the heather afire, kindling a blaze which no man can extinguish ?" [24]

At the obvious risk of sounding repetitious, I want to repeat the thesis of this book which is simple but profound. With notably rare exceptions, the Church in America and the West has lost its fire. Don't get me wrong. It isn't that we don't

". . . much of what passes for "fire" in the Church today is little more than 'fire on ice.'"

have the appearance of fire in the Church, but in the analogy offered by W. T. Stead at the outset of the great Welsh Revival of 1904, much of what passes for "fire" in the Church today is little more than "fire on ice." Such fire is pretty - even spectacular - to watch. And it can be mildly entertaining to the bored and dwindling masses who come to our productions. But the masses came to our Churches expecting to find the fire of God's Presence. Unfortunately, what they found (more often than not) was warmed over and re-packaged religious behavior and second rate special effects. And what little "fire on ice" was present was tightly controlled by those who created it, thereby dooming it to eventual extinction. It never posed any real threat of burning "out of control."

---

[24]William Thomas Stead, ***Christian World***, London, December 15, 1904.

The Inextinguishable Blaze

From the pulpit to the pew the Church of our day is devoid of God's Presence and *"the Inextinguishable Blaze"* of his Holiness which surrounds Him. Holiness is the atmosphere of heaven, produced by the very breath of the Holy One Who rules there. This explains why, when the winds of heaven blow upon the things of this world in seasons of genuine revival and spiritual awakening, men and women breathe that rarified air and a fresh sense of God's holiness grips both the Church and the watching, unbelieving world. Any alleged spiritual awakening that is not characterized by holiness and does not produce a renewed sense of holiness among the participants should be immediately suspect. God is holy, and so is everything He produces.

Isaiah understood this reality. His own experience had taught Him that, when God is present, bushes burn and water boils with holy fire(Isaiah 64:1-2). When He is absent, Churches decorate their stages with artificial shrubbery while giving lip service to a Presence they have never really encountered and which poses no real threat to their artificial stage props. Our worship songs sing about a Presence we know little or nothing about. In the words of A. W. Tozer, *"Christians don't tell lies; they just go to church and sing them."* Yes, we do.

But worst of all, these "fire on ice" sideshows present no serious threat to the fires of secular revolution which now enthrall our Postmodern culture, Hypnotizing the masses to believe that their hope for a better life lies in the next election, or the next political revolution. The crying need of the Church in these opening decades of the 21st Century is to recover the genuine fire of God's Presence and

> "these 'fire on ice' sideshows present no serious threat to the fires of secular revolution which now enthrall our Postmodern culture . . ."

Children Of The Burning Heart

holiness, and to demonstrate to our skeptical secular world the genuine fires of spiritual awakening.

Becoming A People of "The Inextinguishable Blaze"

"The Church is looking for better methods;
God is looking for better men." - E.M. Bounds

E. M. Bounds was right. God is looking for better men. To be more specific, God is looking for men (and women) willing to be carriers of *"the Inextinguishable Blaze*," human kindling for the fire of His Presence and holiness. When we ask the question, *"What does it mean for God to restore His Presence to His Church?"* the inescapable answer is that He is looking for people whom He can use. As in every generation when God has done great things, He begins with a handful of people - *"children of the burning heart"* - who are willing to pursue Him on His terms before the masses ever know what those terms are. Even now, He is calling these *"children of the burning heart"* to seek His holiness and fear, to seek Him in genuine personal repentance and to discover an intimacy with Him that even they never imagined possible. In His call to this generation God is making no distinction between "leaders" and "lay people." He is simply calling His people - whosoever will - regardless of their position or status.

This call to the Church has been growing more intense lately. It is quickly becoming a shout to anyone who will listen. God is sending a clarion call to his Laodicean church in these opening decades of the 21st Century. And just as He did for those lethargic, lukewarm believers in 1st Century Laodicea, when God wants to get our attention and communicate His will, He will find a way, even if He must use angels to do it.

And that's the next story I will tell in the next Chapter.

The Inextinguishable Blaze

Chapter 4

What The Angels Said

Everything we have discussed up to this point should be well known to any serious student of the Scriptures as well as to students of historic spiritual awakenings. Ideas such as God's holiness or the need for personal repentance are clear biblical teachings, and their validity is timeless. In other words, there is NEVER a time when God isn't holy or that He isn't concerned about holiness. There is NEVER a time when genuine personal repentance isn't necessary for a believer or

". . . it is very difficult for an unholy and unrepentant Church to call others to repent."

when it shouldn't be a part of our spiritual lives. The problem with such concepts is that we forget them. We neglect to teach them. We fail to take them seriously. And before long our worship of God no longer includes them and we no longer believe them. And at some unspecified point that no one can identify, what began as our neglect became our idolatry as we began to think, imagine and teach things about God which were not true . . . and we simply went on from there. The Church forgot and abandoned God's holiness, neglected its own holiness and dropped repentance from its vocabulary. After all, it is very difficult for an unholy and unrepentant Church to call others to repent. And things that should have been remembered were quickly forgotten.

It is at times like these, when the Church is out of plumb and the whole structure is in genuine danger of collapse that God

The Inextinguishable Blaze

Himself intervenes in order to reveal what is wrong and to prepare the way for what He wants to do.[25]

Every Vision Needs A Warning

When the New Testament opens up upon 1st Century Judaism after 400 years of biblical silence (since the book of Malachi) it reveals a bankrupt religious structure that God Himself had a hard time recognizing. The 612 commandments of the Law given to Moses had been

"As God began to speak to His remnant and to prepare them for a new visitation, He chose to use His most reliable servants. Angels."

morphed into some 5,000 religious rules (the "traditions of the Elders") which held God's people in religious bondage. It was seriously out of plumb and on the verge of collapse. As God began to speak to His remnant and to prepare them for a new visitation, He chose to use His most reliable servants. Angels. In the New Testament, when God had a special task or message for an individual or a group, he frequently employed angels. Consider a few examples:

1. An angel appeared to Mary to announce the coming of Jesus (Luke 1:26)
2. An angel appeared to Joseph to encourage him to take Mary as his wife (Matt. 1:20)
3. An angel appeared to Zacharias to announce the birth of John the Baptist (Luke 1:11)
4. An angel warned Joseph about Herod (Matt 2:23, and later told Joseph when it was safe to return from Egypt.

---

[25]The letters of the Risen Christ to the Seven Churches of Asia in Revelation 2-3 are our strongest biblical example of this principle at work.

What The Angels Said

5. Angels announced the birth of Jesus to the Shepherds and serenaded them with the first "Christmas Carols"! (Luke 2:9)
6. An angel engineered a "jail break" for the Apostles (Acts 5:19) and later for Peter (Acts 12:7).
7. An angel appeared to a Gentile Roman Centurion named Cornelius and told him to send for Peter to hear the gospel (Acts 10:3, 7 & 22).

I could list more, but you get the point. In the New Testament God used angels extensively whenever he had a special task to complete or a special message to deliver. In order to maintain a healthy spiritual balance, scripture warns believers against undue emphasis upon angels (Colossians 2:18), and such warnings need to be taken seriously (Please read that sentence again!). But such warnings are intended to deliver us from potential error (worshiping angels or giving them unhealthy attention), not to prevent or discourage us from recognizing the truth of how God frequently works.

I have gone to the effort of laying this biblical foundation because what I am about to relate will be a paradigm bender for many of you. Without proper biblical perspective your tendency might be to dismiss what follows as "unbiblical foolishness." As a "recovering rationalist" with a

"In the New Testament God used angels extensively whenever he had a special task to complete or a special message to deliver."

graduate degree in Christian apologetics from an Evangelical Seminary, I understand. Others of you will respond with what I can only describe as a "fatal familiarity," characterized by an attitude of *"Oh, yeah, been there, done that. No big deal."* For these, their familiarity with the supernatural will prove "fatal" due to their failure to appreciate the gravity of what occurred.

The Inextinguishable Blaze

There is a large kernel of wisdom behind the ol' adage that "familiarity breeds contempt." In order to appreciate the significance of what I am about to relate, you will need to avoid both extremes.

A Prayer Meeting That Became A Visitation

Not too long ago several individuals involved in our house church network gathered in the living room of my home in the Spokane Valley for an impromptu prayer gathering. We had no agenda or expectations except to spend some time in prayer seeking God and lifting up the needs of our extended fellowship. There was no sense of anything unusual in the air. I know and trust the people involved. They are house church friends and elders, and people not given to "pushing the envelope" or "flights of fancy." Unknown to us as we began, our unplanned impromptu prayer meeting would last four hours. What I am about to relate began roughly an hour into the gathering. According to four of the eight people who were present and actually witnessed this,[26] three angels appeared, each bearing a specific message.

The First Angel. According to those present who witnessed this, the first angel was clothed in crimson and purple and had a regal nature about him. His message, as recorded by one person present, was as follows:

"This is what the spirit has to say to the 1st Church: Listen! The 1st angel of the church first established in the Lord says this. Repent, for my heart is broken, for I have broken the staff of correction over the backs of my sheep who long for different pastures and whose heart is fat on that which is not

---

[26]I did not personally see the angelic visitors, but I felt their presence in an overwhelming way that I cannot adequately describe.

What The Angels Said

holy, for I will now let them pursue their own lusts and (I will now) stand out of the way!"

The Second Angel. According to those who witnessed this, the second angel was clothed humbly and "non-descriptly" with simple robes. His message was as follows:

"The 2nd angel has to say in a still small voice, be quiet, for only those who seek to drink from the still small brook and who are not afraid of persecution, who love the Lord more than life and thirst not for the glory and the big things that profit only the flesh, who hunger for intimacy, shall enter in! For in such is true power found - in the quiet clearings where the River of God's brook quietly murmurs shall peace and purpose be found. Clothe yourselves in humility, for I shall be found there in peace and tranquility!"

The Third Angel. The third angel was . . . well . . . read on:

"When the 3rd angel approached me I trembled in fear (!) for he is an all consuming fire. His eyes are ablaze with God's glory and his robes are a burning furnace - for he is fresh from the Lord's Presence, shrouded with His glory and holiness! And his presence is a terrible thing, for he has to say: 'Go tell my people to Repent, for they have lost their fear of the Lord, they no longer desire to hear what He truly has to say (It will cost you everything!). Holiness - Holiness - Holiness. Be Holy, for I am holy! Tremble in fear for I am coming!'"

Three "Planks"

As you might expect, everyone who participated in this meeting (yes, I'll go out on a limb and call it a "visitation") was deeply affected both then and for days - even weeks - afterwards. One of them called me several days later on the verge of tears, *"I've been pondering this all day. Maurice, what does this mean?"* Good question. I believe it means several things, but I want to try and summarize what I think is happening in a couple of basic points.

God spoke to us - and is speaking to His Church - in a way very similar to the way He spoke to the Seven Churches of Asia in Revelation. His word is dramatic, specific, challenging and designed to get our attention. Throughout Scripture angelic appearances for the purpose of delivering messages are always significant events. It is like placing an exclamation point at the end of a divine sentence; like driving a stake in the ground so we will not forget or take lightly what He has said. Such visitations are intended to emphasize the *"gravitas"* of both the moment and the message.

As I have reflected on the messages of the three angels I have come to the conclusion (and the other participants agree) that the Holy Spirit was communicating the heart of God for the coming spiritual awakening as expressed in three basic principles or "planks" (i.e., the "boards") God wants to "build" with in the coming spiritual awakening.

Plank # 1 - Holiness And the Fear of God. God is calling His Church to recover a genuine sense of His holiness, and in the process He intends to return *"the fear of the Lord"* to the Church. I regard this as both a call and a promise. God is calling His Church to pursue Him, and at the same time He is promising to visit His Church in "holiness and fear." Such a divine calling and promise represents a terrible but needed "gift" to a Church seriously out of plumb concerning the essential nature of the God they claim to worship. The Church has lost both its holiness and its fear of God. For our part, God wants us to pursue it. For His part, God plans to restore it.

What The Angels Said

Plank # 2 - Genuine Personal Repentance. In recent years personal repentance from sin has become "the lost heart of the Church." In the coming spiritual awakening, God intends to change this. God is once again calling His people to genuine personal repentance, just as He did for the wayward believers of the Seven Churches of Asia, where "repent" is the most common command after "listen." But there is a somber cautionary note contained in the angelic messages. God has been calling His people to repent, but they have resisted the "staff of correction." In response to their failure to repent, God is preparing to send them one of the worst forms of judgment in all of Scripture. For some of His sheep He is about to give them what they want. He is going to stand aside and let them have their own way: *"I will now let them pursue their own lusts and (I will now) stand out of the way!"* It is a terrible day in the life of any professing believer or church when God gives them over to the lusts and desires of their own heart because they refused to repent when commanded and given the opportunity to do so.

Plank # 3 - Intimacy. In this third plank God is calling His people to quietude and listening to His still small voice. I believe this speaks of pursuing humility and intimacy with God. God wants an intimate people. But genuine intimacy with God must be preceded by holiness and fear, followed by genuine personal repentance from sin as God's holiness reveals it. If taken seriously, this plank will force a very busy, distracted and self-absorbed Western Church to ask a very basic question: *"Are we listening, or are we too busy pursuing 'great things' to hear God's still small voice which can only be heard in times of humility and intimacy with Him?"*

Making Sense of It All

I believe that God's Church in the West is on the eve of a

The Inextinguishable Blaze

profound season of divine visitation and historic Spiritual Awakening. For this reason He has chosen to "drive a stake in the ground" - one of those *"Remember this day!"* kind of moments. He is calling His Church to actively pursue His holiness and fear, genuine personal repentance, and a deeper intimacy with Himself. These three messages are not new, either to Scripture or to God's Church through the ages. But they appear to be new to the Church in the opening decades of the 21st Century. Which explains why He is giving them special attention now.

The Inextinguishable Blaze

It is time for the Church of God to listen and to hear what the Spirit is saying to the Church of our generation. As He did for the Churches of Asia in Revelation 2-3 He is telling us, *"I am coming."* He is preparing us for a visitation of His Spirit that will manifest in holiness and fear, genuine personal repentance and intimacy with Him. The only real question is whether or not we are willing to pursue and embrace it on His terms.

Are we?

"A true love of God must begin with a delight in his holiness." - Jonathan Edwards

"There is no shortcut to holiness; it must be the business of our whole lives." - William Wilberforce

"Cowards never won heaven. Do not claim that you are begotten of God and have His royal blood running in your veins unless you can prove your lineage by this heroic spirit: to dare to be holy in spite of men and devils." - William Gurnall

"It is not great talents or great learning or great preachers that God needs, but men great in holiness." - E. M. Bounds

"God has one destined end for mankind - holiness! His one aim is the production of saints. God is not an eternal blessing- machine for men. He did not come to save men out of pity. He came to save men because He had created them to be holy." - Oswald Chambers

"Whatever call a man may pretend to have, if he has not been called to holiness, he certainly has not been called to the ministry." - Charles H. Spurgeon

"Many Christians have what we might call a 'cultural holiness'. They adapt to the character and behavior pattern of Christians around them. As the Christian culture around them is more or less holy, so these Christians are more or less holy. But God has not called us to be like those around us. He has called us to be like Himself. Holiness is nothing less than conformity to the character of God." - Jerry Bridges

61

The Inextinguishable Blaze

"Christ will be master of the heart, and sin must be mortified. If your life is unholy, then your heart is unchanged, and you are an unsaved person. The Saviour will sanctify His people, renew them, give them a hatred of sin, and a love of holiness. The grace that does not make a man better than others is a worthless counterfeit. Christ saves His people, not IN their sins, but FROM their sins. Without holiness, no man shall see the Lord." - Charles Spurgeon

"We have learned to live with unholiness and have come to look upon it as the natural and expected thing." - A. W. Tozer

"Why are we not more holy? Chiefly because we are enthusiasts, looking for the end without the means." - John Wesley

"An unholy church! It is useless to the world, and of no esteem among men. It is an abomination, hell's laughter, heaven's abhorrence. The worst evils which have ever come upon the world have been brought upon her by an unholy church." - C.H. Spurgeon

"It is an undoubted truth that every doctrine that comes from God, leads to God; and that which doth not tend to promote holiness is not of God." - George Whitefield

Chapter 5

Understanding Biblical Holiness

"If one were asked to describe in a word the outstanding feature of those days, one would unhesitatingly reply that it was the universal, inescapable sense of the presence of God. Revival is the exact answer to such a sigh as that of Isaiah 64:1, 'Oh that Thou wouldst rend the heavens, that Thou wouldst come down, that the mountains might flow down at Thy presence.' In 1904 the Lord had literally rent the heavens, and had scattered the satanic foes entrenched therein. The Lord had come down! The mountains were gloriously melted down in His presence." [27]

During the Great Welsh Revival of 1904 participants soon became aware of several things. As Jones described above, the first thing they noticed was the overwhelming sense of the pervasive Presence of God. But they soon noticed something else, a phenomenon which came to characterize the revival, even to outside observers. They began to notice numerous and repeated acts of "practical holiness" which broke out spontaneously throughout South Wales.

For example, as the revival swept the coal mines of Wales, cursing and profanity among the notoriously profane miners fell dramatically. Profanity was so reduced that coal production nearly came to a complete halt. So many miners were converted (or at least convicted) and gave up profanity and cursing that the pit ponies which pulled the coal cars in the mine tunnels could no longer understand the new verbal commands. Work slowed down until the bewildered creatures could adjust to the new reality of practical and personal

---

[27] R. B. Jones, **Rent Heavens** (Porth, Wales: South Wales Bible Training Institute, 1931).

holiness.

But there was more. The holiness of God's Presence brought about genuine repentance in the lives of people and found expression through practical deeds. Longstanding debts were repaid, stolen goods were returned, and cases of restitution for past sins and grievances became so frequent as to be noteworthy. In the Welsh village of Maesteg a businessman received a live pig in payment of a debt which had been outstanding for some six (6) years. In some jurisdictions judges were issued white gloves signifying no cases to try as crime all but vanished. In Glamorgan County the number of illegitimate births fell by 44% in the year following the outbreak of the revival. In the city of Swansea, the "Poor Law Guardians," who administered relief to the poor, commented on the unusual number of working people who had come to take their aged parents home from the workhouses to which they had been sent. [28]

> *"The holiness of God's Presence brought about genuine repentance in the lives of people and found expression through practical deeds."*

The point here is simple, practical, and could be illustrated with examples from other historic spiritual awakenings. When the Presence of God visits a place and a people, the fire of His Presence brings with it an irresistible sense of His holiness. The fire of God's holiness touches people, ignites in them *"the Inextinguishable Blaze"* of His holiness, and

---

[28] J. Edwin Orr, *The Flaming Tongue: The Impact of Twentieth Century Revivals* (Chicago: Moody Press, 1973). page 18.

Understanding Biblical Holiness

manifests itself in what is best described as acts of "practical holiness." Our holiness is the product of His holiness. The fire of His holiness ignites a fire of holiness in us. We become holy because He is holy.

"When the Presence of God visits a place and a people, the fire of His Presence brings with it an irresistible sense of His holiness."

Having said this, we are now forced to answer the basic question that you should have asked by now (if you haven't asked it already): What is holiness?

The Idea of The Holy

Let's get started by dealing with the answer of the philosophers and the theologians first. Rudolf Otto was a German theologian of the early 20th century. In 1917 he published what would become his most famous work, entitled *The Idea of the Holy*.[29] It became one of the most successful German theological books of the 20th century. It has never gone out of print and is now available in some twenty languages. Otto defined the concept of "the holy" as that which is "numinous,"[30] by which he meant a *"non-rational, non-sensory experience or feeling whose primary and immediate object is outside the self."* He defined

---

[29]That was its simplified English title. It was originally published in German as **Das Heilige - Über das Irrationale in der Idee des Göttlichen und sein Verhältnis zum Rationalen** or **The Holy - On the Irrational in the Idea of the Divine and its Relation to the Rational.**

[30]Latin: *"a fearful and fascinating mystery."* The term "numinous" is an English adjective, taken from the Latin *numen*, meaning "divinity," or "divine presence" and used to describe the power or presence of the "divine."

The Inextinguishable Blaze

the "numinous" as a *mysterium tremendum et fascinans*. For Otto, both religion and "the holy" could be reduced to an undiscoverable presence which *"runs like quicksilver through creation's veins."*

Rudolf Otto's concept of the "numinous" makes for interesting - even required - reading among theology students and budding philosophers. But it offers little in the way of practical guidance for a Church in search of moral and spiritual renewal. The good news is that the "undiscoverable presence" that Otto attempted to write about is, in realty, the personal Presence of The Holy One of Israel, Whose Presence not only *"runs like quicksilver through creation's veins,"* but Who both transcends His creation and sets the hearts and minds of men on fire with *"the Inextinguishable Blaze"* of His Presence and holiness. Just ask J. Edwin Orr.

Until his home-going in 1987, Dr. J. Edwin Orr was widely regarded as the "dean" of revival students everywhere. In lectures delivered for Campus Crusade for Christ at Purdue University in the 1970s Dr. Orr recounted his experience at a student conference led by Dr. Henrietta Mears at Forest Home Conference Center in California in August of 1949. Dr. Orr recounts how, late one evening, he received a knock on the door of his room. When he opened the door there stood a young evangelist who had just returned from a long walk in the woods during which he had experienced a profound encounter with the Presence of God. William Franklin Graham had been personally touched by the profound Presence of God. That encounter brought Graham to the end of what had been an ongoing crisis of faith. Graham surrendered himself to the Presence and renewed his commitment to the Bible as the inspired word of God. The fire of God's Presence now rested upon a young Billy Graham. The following month Graham began his now-famous Greater Los Angeles Crusade which launched his nationwide public

Understanding Biblical Holiness

evangelistic ministry. For Billy Graham, as for so many saints before him, the "numinous" indescribable "presence" which Rudolf Otto labored to understand had manifested Himself in the Person of the Holy One of Israel Who ignites the hearts of men and sets them on fire with *"the Inextinguishable Blaze"* of His Presence and holiness.

So, What Is Holiness?

I would dare say that most Christians (and many non-Christians) confuse "holiness" with some form of legalism and rule keeping, something along the line of *"I don't dance, drink, smoke or chew or run around with girls*

"Genuine holiness . . . . is about Who you worship, Who you love and Whose image is transforming your life."

(or boys) who do." Let's be clear from the outset. Genuine holiness isn't about what music you listen to (or don't listen to), what clothes you wear, whether or not you wear jewelry, what books you read or movies you watch, or how much (or little) money you have. Such externals (and I could have listed many more) have no direct bearing upon genuine holiness although genuine holiness may have an effect on all those things. An unbeliever could abstain from all those external things and still not be "holy" in any genuine biblical sense. Religious legalism and rule keeping represent the counterfeit currency of the Church - fool's gold. It cannot be spent in the Kingdom of God, but it has frequently been used by religious legalists throughout the ages to ensnare many a seeker after righteousness.

Genuine holiness, on the other hand, is about Who you worship, Who you love and Whose image is transforming your life. Holiness begins with God and ends with us being transformed into His image. Because of Who you love (or fail

The Inextinguishable Blaze

to love) you can be holy in a dung pile, or unholy in a church meeting. True and genuine holiness has nothing to do with those external things. Genuine holiness begins with the fire of God's Presence and holiness in our hearts and works its way outward through personal confession and repentance into the totality of our lives, not the other way around.[31] That's the fools gold of legalism. Don't even try to spend it with a God Who knows better, Who describes Himself as an assayer of metals and tester of men's hearts (Psalm 66:10; Isaiah 48:10; Zechariah 13:9; Psalm 11:4).

When it comes to understanding God's holiness, biblical word studies on the vocabulary of holiness can only take us so far, but that's where we will begin. The Hebrew word-stem for holiness (*Kadesh* - *qds*) is understood by scholars as having two essential meanings. The first is the idea of

> *"Holiness is that quality of God's essential nature whereby He is totally and completely separated from sin and is singularly devoted to His own glory."*

"separation" and refers to something which is cut off, separate or set apart, in a category all its own. *Kadesh* describes something that is separated or set apart from the sphere of what is ordinary. [32] As we will discover moving forward, biblical separation involves both a separation "from"

---

[31]This is Jesus' point in Matthew 15:1-20. Men defile themselves and lose their "holiness" from the inside out.

[32]The New Testament word *hagios* also means set apart, separate and so in a class by itself. It follows that for believers the call to be holy is a call to be separated from common use and set apart, or reserved, for special use.

Understanding Biblical Holiness

and a separation "to." The second meaning involves the idea of something that is *"bright, brilliant, radiant or pure,"* which leads to the idea of something so brilliant, so pure and so "beautiful" as to be *"terrifying."* And that's as far as word definitions can carry us. Everything else we need to know or will ever learn about holiness must come from how the Scriptures use this word-group with respect to God, people, places and things.

At the risk of being premature, I want to offer a working definition of holiness which the remainder of our study will demonstrate. Holiness is that quality of God's essential nature whereby He is totally and completely separated from sin and is singularly devoted to His own glory. At the same time, holiness is that pure, brilliant, beautiful and penetrating light of God's presence which exposes our sin for the terrible rebellion and offense against God it truly is. How terrible is sin? So terrible that the wrath of God Himself is reserved for one thing and one thing only - the punishment of sin. God responds to sin as a personal affront to His holiness. In a very real and biblical sense, holiness is "personal," not "legal," and that is where we want to begin.

1. Holiness Is A Person

"And one cried unto another, and said, Holy, holy, holy, is the LORD of hosts: the whole earth is full of his glory." (Isaiah 6:3)

Certain passages of Scripture represent pivotal moments in our understanding of spiritual reality. This passage from the sixth chapter of Isaiah is one of those passages

"Some things may be 'holy', and a few things may be 'most holy,' but only God is 'holy, holy, holy.'"

The Inextinguishable Blaze

and one of those moments in our understanding of God's holiness. I will treat this passage in greater detail later in Chapter 11, but for now I want to offer an observation about the relationship of holiness to God's essential nature. This is one of those times when human vocabulary struggles with the task of communicating the reality of the Divine nature. The Hebrew language regularly uses repetition for emphasis. Over 430 times the Hebrew Old Testament refers to people or things as "holy" (a single use of the word _qds_). Some 43 times the Hebrew text refers to things, places or people as "most holy." It does this by repeating the word _qds_ (literally: "holy, holy"). But only God is referred to as "holy, holy, holy." Some things may be "holy', and a few things may be "most holy," but only God is _"holy, holy, holy."_[33]

Here is the observation and the point. No other attribute or characteristic of God's nature is ever referred to this way. While Scripture tells us that "God is love," no where are we ever told that God is "love, love, love." God and holiness are

> _"God and holiness are synonymous and inseparable in a way that defies description except for the seraphim to cry, 'holy, holy, holy.'"_

synonymous and inseparable in a way that defies description except for the seraphim to cry, "holy, holy, holy." It would be wrong for us to conclude that "holy" or "holiness" simply describes one of God's many wonderful characteristics or attributes. Rather, this is what philosophers and theologians would characterize as an "existential" statement: one that

---

[33]To avoid any urge to dismiss this passage as a "fluke" of the Old Testament we should point out that the Apostle John tells us in Revelation 4:8 that the angels who worship around God's throne repeat the declaration of "holy, holy, holy." Even in the New Testament, holiness continues to define God's essential nature.

Understanding Biblical Holiness

defines God's very existence, the very nature of His essential being. God *IS* holy. We can define "holiness" with one word: God. Holiness is the essential nature of Who God is. Just as the Name of God (*"I am that I am"*), which He revealed to Moses at the burning bush, expressed His self-existent nature (see Exodus 3:19), so holiness expresses His essential moral nature. *"Holy is the way God is,"* writes Tozer. *"To be holy He does not conform to a standard. He is that standard. He is absolutely holy with an infinite, incomprehensible fullness of purity that is incapable of being other than it is."* [34]

Throughout the years Christian writers have wrestled with the challenge of adequately communicating the biblical idea of God's holiness. Listen to the words of A. W. Pink:

"This perfection, as none other, is solemnly celebrated before the Throne of Heaven, the seraphim crying, 'Holy, holy, holy, is the Lord of hosts' (Isa. 6:3). God Himself singles out this perfection, 'Once have I sworn by my holiness' (Ps. 89:35). God swears by His holiness because that is a fuller expression of Himself than anything else. Therefore are we exhorted, 'Sing unto the Lord, O ye saints of His, and give thanks at the remembrance of His holiness' (Ps. 30:4). 'This may be said to be a transcendental attribute, that, as it were, runs through the rest, and casts luster upon them. It is an attribute of attributes' (J. Howe, 1670). Thus we read of 'the beauty of the Lord' (Ps. 27:4), which is none other than 'the beauty of holiness'" (Ps. 110:3).[35]

---

[34]A. W. Tozer, *The Knowledge of the Holy*, page 113.

[35]A. W. Pink - *The Attributes of God*, Chapter 8: *The Holiness of God*.

The Inextinguishable Blaze

God is holy. Holiness is a Person.

God In His Holiness Is A Consuming Fire

It bears repeating that human language and vocabulary struggle to communicate what the human mind cannot fathom, namely, a moral brilliance and purity unlike anything we have ever known. One so brilliant, pure and beautiful as to be "terrifying." And one of the ways the biblical writers have attempted to describe the moral brilliance and purity of God's holiness has been to describe Him as "a consuming fire." Consider these words from the Prophet Isaiah:

> *"Sinners in Zion are terrified;*
> *Trembling has seized the godless.*
> *'Who among us can live with the consuming fire?*
> *Who among us can live with continual burning?'"*
> (Isaiah 33:14)

On nine different occasions Scripture describes God as "a consuming fire."[36] Why? Perhaps because fire both consumes and purifies. While the most familiar of these passages is found in the New Testament in Hebrews 12:29,

"God is holy. Holiness is a Person. And the holiness of His Presence is 'a consuming fire.'"

the writer of Hebrews is merely reiterating the declaration of Moses in Deuteronomy, *"For the LORD your God is a consuming fire, a jealous God"* (Deuteronomy 4:24). In His holiness, the self-existent God of Scripture is "a consuming fire." And when this God Who is a holy, consuming fire,

---

[36]Exodus 24:17, Deuteronomy 4:24 & 9:3; Isaiah 29:6; 30:27 & 30; 33:14; Lamentations 2:3; Hebrews 12:29

Understanding Biblical Holiness

touches men and women as Isaiah was touched with a burning coal from the altar, He sets their hearts ablaze with holy fire. In the process, the fire of God's holiness and Presence accomplishes at least three things: it consumes, it purifies . . . and it spreads.

God is holy. Holiness is a Person. And the holiness of His Presence is "a consuming fire."

God in His Holiness Is Transcendent

"Who is like unto thee, O LORD, among the gods? Who is like thee, glorious in holiness, fearful in praises, doing wonders?" (Exodus 15:11)

Welcome to the biblical language of "transcendence." This verse from Exodus is just one of many biblical passages which ring with the biblical language of transcendence. When we say that God is transcendent what we mean is that He is both greater than and separated from His creation. He transcends it. God's "transcendence" has led philosophers and theologians to coin a phrase to capture and express the idea: God in His transcendence is *"the Other."*

." . . *we must not compare the being of God with any other. This would be to grant God eminence, even pre-eminence, but that is not enough; we must grant Him transcendence in the fullest meaning of that word. Forever God stands apart, in light unapproachable."* [37]

Creation may indeed declare the greatness and the glory of God (Psalms 8 & 19), but God is greater than and more glorious than His creation. He rules over creation. Creation

---

[37]Tozer, *The Knowledge of The Holy*, page 76

does not rule Him. He was great and glorious as the self-existent One before He spoke that Word which created everything that now is. God is God without His creation, but His creation is nothing without Him. In Him we live and move and have our being. God still speaks through His Creation. And even in its present fallen condition it responds to His commands. He bends it to His will, sometimes in events so spectacular that men refer to them as miracles. *"Who, indeed, is like unto Thee, O God,"* must be the continual cry of the worshiping human heart.

We can sympathize with a Rudolf Otto who wrestles with words to describe God's holiness and can only describe it as "a *mysterium* *tremendum* *et* *fascinans*." To say that God is more glorious than His creation, as the sun is more glorious than the moon, is to insult and belittle the sun and to exalt the moon beyond all reason. God in His glorious holiness is transcendent above His creation to a degree that humbles our pride, strikes fear into our hearts, impoverishes our language and strains human vocabulary to its breaking point. *"Who is like Thee, O God, glorious in holiness, fearful in praises, doing wonders?"*

God is holy. Holiness is a Person. God in His glorious holiness is "transcendent."

God in His Holiness Is Separated

We could have simply included this idea of separation under the idea of transcendence, but I think it deserves a separate-but-brief treatment. God in His holiness is separated from His creation which has fallen into sin and stands in need of redemption. God is not so separated from His creation as to be uninvolved (as taught by Deism), nor is God so identified with His creation as to be synonymous with it (as in Eastern religious thought, including monism, pantheism and panentheism). This truth is in keeping with the definition of holiness we offered earlier: Holiness is that quality of God's essential nature whereby He is totally and completely separated from sin and is singularly devoted to His own glory. At the same time, holiness is that pure, brilliant and penetrating light of God's presence which exposes our sin for the terrible rebellion and offense against God it truly is. It is God's holiness and separation from His fallen creation, along with its crying need for redemption, which forms the basis for His plan for redemption and salvation in and through Christ.

God is holy. Holiness is a Person. God in His glorious holiness is separated from His creation.

God in His Holiness Is Beautiful

We saw earlier that the meaning of the Hebrew word for holiness (*qds*) includes the idea of something that is *"bright, brilliant, radiant or pure"* which leads to the idea of something so brilliant, so pure and so beautiful as to be "terrifying." Consider the problem here confronting the biblical writer. How do we describe the beauty of something, or more properly "Someone," which is beyond description, a beauty so bright, so brilliant and so pure as to be "terrifying." There is a danger here of attempting to compare God-in-his-holiness with earthly things we already know. And yet, God in His holiness is unlike ANYTHING we know. And there's the dilemma. We can never understand God's holiness by thinking of a person or thing we regard as "pure" and then elevating that person or thing to the *"N"*[th] degree.

"God's holiness is not simply the best we know infinitely bettered. We know nothing like the divine holiness. It stands apart, unique, unapproachable, incomprehensible and unattainable. The natural man is blind to it. He may fear God's power and admire His wisdom, but His holiness he

The Inextinguishable Blaze

cannot even imagine.[38]

In short, God's holiness is a beauty beyond anything we can imagine, but it is just as real as the most beautiful sunset or the most spectacular sunrise. Consider the following passages which refer to the beauty of God's holiness. This is one of those times when the older translators (such as the KJV) more fully catch the sense of the text. Consider the following passages:

*"Give unto the LORD the glory due unto his name: bring an offering, and come before him: worship the LORD in the **beauty of holiness**."* (1 Chronicles 16:29)

*"And when he had consulted with the people, he appointed singers unto the LORD, and that should praise the **beauty of holiness**, as they went out before the army, and to say, Praise the LORD; for his mercy endureth for ever."* (2 Chronicles 20:21)

*"One thing have I desired of the LORD, that will I seek after; that I may dwell in the house of the LORD all the days of my life, to behold the **beauty of the LORD**, and to enquire in his temple."* (Psalm 27:4)

*"Give unto the LORD the glory due unto his name; worship the LORD in the **beauty of holiness**."* (Psalm 29:2)

*"O worship the LORD in the **beauty of holiness**: fear before him, all the earth."* (Psalm 96:9)

*"Thy people shall be willing in the day of thy power, in the **beauties of holiness** from the womb of the morning: thou*

---

[38]Tozer, *The Knowledge of The Holy*, page 111.

Understanding Biblical Holiness

hast the dew of thy youth." (Psalm 110:3)

Simply put, God in His holiness possesses a beauty that is to be worshiped, praised and feared among the people of God. Puritan divine and Presbyterian pastor Stephen Charnock (1628–1680) summarized the beauty of God's holiness this way:

*"The holiness of God is his glory and crown. It is the blessedness of his nature. It renders him glorious in himself, and glorious to his creatures. "Holy" is more fixed as an epithet to his name than any other. This is his greatest title of honor. He is pure and unmixed light, free from all blemish in his essence, nature, and operations. He cannot be deformed by any evil. The notion of God cannot be entertained without separating from him whatever is impure and staining. Though he is majestic, eternal, almighty, wise, immutable, merciful, and whatsoever other prefections may dignify so sovereign a being, yet if we conceive him destitute of this excellent perfection, and imagine him possessed with the least contagion of evil, we make him but an infinite monster, and sully all those perfections we ascribed to him before. It is a contradiction for him to be God and to have any darkness mixed with his light. To deny his purity, makes him no God. He that says God is not holy, speaks much worse than if he said there is no God at all. Where do we read of the angels crying out Eternal or Faithful Lord God of hosts? But we do hear them singing Holy, Holy, Holy. God swears by his holiness (Psa. 89:35). His holiness is a pledge for the assurance of his promises. Power is his hand, omniscience his eye, mercy his heart, eternity his duration, but **holiness his beauty**. It renders him lovely and gives beauty to all his attributes. Every action of his is free from all hints of evil. Holiness is the crown of all his attributes, the life of all his decrees, and the brightness of all his actions. Nothing is decreed by him and nothing is acted by him that is not*

The Inextinguishable Blaze

consistent with the beauty of his holiness." [39]

God is holy. Holiness is a Person. God in His holiness is beautiful beyond description.

Summary. Welcome to *"the Inextinguishable Blaze"* of the God Whose Presence and holiness are *"a consuming fire"* in the midst of His people. The fire of His holiness is personal, not legal or theoretical. In His holiness

> *"God is holy. Holiness is a Person. God in His holiness is beautiful beyond description."*

He transcends His creation and is separate (i.e., "distinct") from it, while bending it to His will and working to redeem it from its fallen condition. And in all that He does in His holiness He manifests a moral purity and brilliance that is both beautiful beyond description and "terrifying" beyond words. He is the God of *"the Inextinguishable Blaze"* Who is calling His people back into a relationship with Himself. And that is where we want to turn next.

2. Holiness Is A Relationship

"I am the LORD who sanctifies you" (Leviticus 20:8).

The truth that *"Holiness is a Person"* leads us to another critical truth: *Holiness is a relationship.* Genuine personal holiness requires a genuine personal relationship with the God Who is "holy, holy, holy." Simply stated, nothing is "holy" - no person, no place, no object, no thing - apart from a relationship with the God Who IS holy. The Hebrew word translated "sanctifies" in the above passage from Leviticus

---

[39]Stephen Charnock, ***The Existence and Attributes of God.***

Understanding Biblical Holiness

(and in the other 9 similar passages) is the verbal form of the same root (*qds*) as "holiness." Literally, the passage should read, *"I am the LORD who makes you holy."* [40]

Older theologians were fond of writing about the doctrine of "prevenience." Simply put, the doctrine of "prevenience" means that God is always "prevenient." God always acts first. The greatest example of this is perhaps God's love. God's love is prevenient, as John reminds us, *"We love (God), because He first loved us."* (1 John 4:19) The same is true of holiness. If holiness is a person - the Person of God - then nothing else can be holy apart from a relationship with Him. And no one can have a relationship with Him unless He acts first. He must sanctify us. God Himself must act to make us holy. God Himself must ignite *"the Inextinguishable Blaze"* of holiness in our hearts.

Our problem and challenge in the Church is that we have too much theological knowledge and too little fire. We have had the fire of God's holiness and presence taught out of us by people who believe that a class which analyzes fire is an acceptable substitute for

> *"When you place the well-being of the Church in the sole keeping of teachers, they will teach the body into a 'coma' of knowledge without fire."*

experiencing fire itself. Racing to the "punchline" of a theological argument, teachers have assured their classes that, since we are in Christ by faith we share His holiness by virtue of His atonement. Therefore, we're all "holy" (or "sanctified") and can move on to thinking about more

---

[40]See also Exodus 31:13; Leviticus 20:8; 21:8, 15, 23; 22:9,16, 32; Ezekiel 20:12; 37:28

The Inextinguishable Blaze

important subjects, like the need for good stewardship and supporting the annual pledge drive. There is a warning here for all of us: When you place the well-being of the Church in the sole keeping of teachers, they will teach the body into a "coma" of knowledge without fire.

But the lesson of Scripture is clear that the fire of God's holiness is personal. He doesn't want to be studied. He wants to be experienced, worshiped, obeyed . . . and spread by carriers of *"the*

"God is holy. Holiness is a Person. Holiness is a Relationship."

Inextinguishable Blaze." Without the consuming fire of God's holiness, there is no fire of holiness in the human heart or in the Church, regardless of how "solid" the teaching might be, or regardless of how many religious rules we might try to keep. This is the truth embodied, not just in the above passage from Leviticus 20:8 and the other Scriptures which repeat this truth. It is the truth embodied in ALL of Scripture. God is holy by nature. We are holy by virtue of our relationship with Him. He is the one who "sanctifies" us (i.e., "makes us holy"). The consuming fire of His holiness consumes us, purifies us and sanctifies us. His fire becomes our fire, borrowed and on loan from His altar, but just as real. By virtue of our relationship with Him we now share"the Inextinguishable Blaze."

God is holy. Holiness is a Person. Holiness is a Relationship.

3. Holiness Is A Calling

"For I am the LORD your God . . . be holy; for I am holy." (Leviticus 11:44; 20:7)

." . *. but like the Holy One who called you, be holy yourselves*

Understanding Biblical Holiness

also in all your behavior; because it is written, 'You shall be holy, for I am holy.'" (1 Peter 1:5)

Old and New Testament saints share a common calling. We have both been called to holiness. We have been called into a relationship with the God Whose Presence is "a consuming fire" of holiness. We have been called to be carriers of "the Inextinguishable Blaze." As New Testament believers we are "holy" by virtue of our saving faith in Jesus, but even we are commanded to "be holy." That fact alone should tell us that there is more to holiness than most of us know or have been taught. Our challenge is to be who we are in Christ yet still pursue the fire and holiness of His Presence. To "be holy" is to become *"children of the burning heart"* who continue to pursue that which we have already found. It is to know and experience the fire of His Presence and holiness, and to become carriers of *"the Inextinguishable Blaze"* in our generation.

We have been called to carry God's fire and to manifest His holiness to our generation. And it is not a calling that can be refused . . . if we desire genuine intimacy with Him. As Tozer observes, *"God is holy with an absolute holiness that knows no degrees, and this He cannot impart to His creatures. But there is a relative and contingent holiness which He shares with angels and seraphim in heaven and with redeemed men on earth as their preparation for heaven. This holiness God can and does impart to His children. He shares it with them by imputation and by impartation, and because He has made it available to them through the blood of the Lamb, **He requires it of them**."* [41]

I know of few biblical believers who would consciously or

---

[41]Tozer, **The Knowledge of The Holy**, page 113.

The Inextinguishable Blaze

intentionally minimize the unconditional love of God as taught in the Scriptures, and rightly so. But the reality is that the Evangelical Church of our generation has in fact minimized God's love to little more than a fig leaf behind which to mask and hide its lack of fire and holiness.

A. W. Tozer observes that ." . . *God's first concern for His universe is its moral health, that is, for its holiness.*" If true, then the Evangelical Church of our generation is in for a rude correction, perhaps even a rude spiritual awakening. In order to preserve the moral and spiritual health of His Church, God must either redeem, renew or destroy whatever would destroy it. And our lack of holiness is currently destroying His Church. For that reason

> *"The Evangelical Church of our generation has in fact minimized God's love to little more than a fig leaf behind which to mask and hide its lack of fire and holiness."*

alone it should come as no surprise that God would act to restore holiness and fear to His Church, just as He has promised. And that truth alone should strike a degree of fear in the heart of the Church of our generation.

The Inextinguishable Blaze

"Follow peace with all, and holiness, without which no one shall see the Lord." (Hebrews 12:14)

"I know your deeds, that you are neither cold nor hot; I would that you were cold or hot. So because you are lukewarm, and neither hot nor cold, I will spit you out of My mouth." (Revelation 3:15-16)

Understanding Biblical Holiness

It is time for the Church of our generation to be honest with itself and with God. It is time for us to confront our lack of fire, our lack of holiness and our lack of the Presence of God in our midst. When the Risen Christ rebuked and admonished the Church of Laodicea, He rebuked them for being lukewarm. Why was their "lukewarmness" so offensive to Jesus? Could it be because there is no such thing as lukewarm fire? It is time for us to repent of our Laodicean lukewarmness and to once again become "children of the burning heart" and bearers of"the Inextinguishable Blaze."

The world of our generation is perishing because it has yet to see the fire and the power of a genuinely holy Church. Are you prepared to show it to them?

The Inextinguishable Blaze

Chapter 6

Be Separate, Or Be Consumed

In the previous chapter we explored the Scriptural teaching that holiness is a person, a relationship and a calling. One of the truths we discovered along the way was that at the heart of biblical holiness is the idea of "separation." Now we want to briefly explore how this principle of "separation" was applied in the life of God's Old Testament people and their relationship with God.

Welcome To Holiness In The Old Testament

If we could summarize now what we are about to discover concerning the principle of "separation" and the fire of God's holiness in the Old Testament, it would be this: "Be separate, or be consumed."

"Holiness in the Old Testament was primarily about physical separation."

Holiness in the Old Testament was primarily about physical separation.[42] The Old Testament teaches, illustrates and emphasizes the seriousness of sin and the high price required to worship a holy God. Part of that high price was expressed and illustrated through elaborate rituals of separation which served to emphasize God's enmity toward and separation from sin. Everything in the daily religious life of Israel was designed by God to emphasize the principle of separation from sin on the one hand and separation to God on the other.

---

[42]While the concept of separation remains in the New Testament word for holiness (*hagios*), the focus of New Testament holiness is primarily upon inward transformation. More about that later.

The Inextinguishable Blaze

Now, a word of reminder and of caution is in order before we proceed. As we discovered in the previous chapter, Holiness is first and foremost "personal," as opposed to "legal." God is Holy, and holiness is a person. If you and I miss this truth then we will become legalists seeking laws, rules, days and feasts to make us "holy" rather than becoming

God was holy in His Person long before He expressed that holiness in the Law. And He remains holy in His person even after the demands of the Law have been fulfilled in Christ.

worshipers seeking the holiness of God's Presence. We will make the categorical mistake of confusing the keeping of rules with a genuine relationship with God. God was holy in His Person long before He expressed that holiness in the Law. And He remains holy in His person even after the demands of the Law have been fulfilled in Christ. Holiness is a Person and "a consuming fire." The only way you will ever get "fire" out of a set of rules is to use a box of matches.

In His person, God's holiness is "a consuming fire," not a set of laws and rules to be obeyed. The purpose of His rules and laws as laid out in the 612 requirements of the Law, and all of the religious rituals and ordinances of separation, was to remind His people of the extent of His holiness, and to keep them from being consumed by the fire of His Presence as they went about their daily lives with the Presence of God in their midst.

God in His holiness set aside a people for His purposes.
God's holiness in the Old Testament began with God separating out a nation or people for himself from among all others. They would be His unique possession, which meant they would be holy, just as He is holy:

Be Separate, Or Be Consumed

"Now then, if you will indeed obey My voice and keep My covenant, then you shall be My own possession among all the peoples, for all the earth is Mine; and you shall be to Me a kingdom of priests and a holy nation. These are the words that you shall speak to the sons of Israel." (Exodus 19:5-6)

"Thus you are to be holy to Me, for I the LORD am holy; and I have set you apart from the peoples to be Mine." (Leviticus 20:26; see also 20:24)

This meant that the people of God as a group would be holy, set apart by God and for God. This principle would carry over to the New Testament as well. There is only one people of God, people who by calling, redemption and faith have been set aside by God for His purposes. And part of their common calling is to share the fire of His holiness.

God in His holiness set aside groups of people for His purposes. The entire priestly-tabernacle service, from the people who administered it to the objects which were a part of it, provided a living daily demonstration of the seriousness of holiness as expressed through the principle of "separation." Here are just a few examples of people who were set aside in exclusive roles:

1) The Levites - The Levites were the tribe which God set aside ("separated") for the sole purpose of ministering to Him and serving the tabernacle. Their encampment surrounded the Tabernacle.(see Numbers 3)

2) The Priests - They were members of the tribe of Levi, but more specifically they were the sons and descendants of Aaron. (Numbers 3:1-3) The Priests camped on the east side of the Tabernacle and guarded its entrance. (Numbers 3:38-39)

The Inextinguishable Blaze

3) The Kohathites - The Kohathites were Levites who camped on the south side of the Tabernacle and were responsible for carrying the contents of the Tabernacle whenever it was time to move. (Numbers 3:27-32)

4) The Merarites - This Clan of Levites camped on the north side of the Tabernacle and was responsible for carrying the structural frame and components of the tabernacle. (Numbers 3:33-37)

5) The Gershonites - This Clan of Levites camped on the west side of the Tabernacle and was responsible for carrying the coverings, hangings and screens of the Tabernacle. (Numbers 3:21-26)

In the Old Testament God's holiness allowed for no flexibility in these assigned roles. In Numbers 16, when a Levite named Korah (a Kohathite) demanded to be allowed to perform priestly duties on the basis that all the Levites, as well as all the people, are equally holy, the response of God in His holiness was to destroy Korah, his family and all of his co-complainers and their families. God in His holiness was not known for His flexibility.

The principle at work was simple, profound and inescapable: *"Be separate, or be consumed."* Failure to observe and keep all of the rules of separation represented a failure to treat and honor God as holy in the eyes of the people - a public challenge to God's holiness. While the punishment for violating this principle could

"Holiness is a person. Our disobedience to His revealed will represents a personal affront to the God Whose Presence and holiness are 'a consuming fire.'"

Be Separate, Or Be Consumed

vary, it applied to everyone. Even to Moses and Aaron. In Numbers 20, when Moses struck the rock rather than speaking to it as instructed by God, he and Aaron violated this basic principle. God's response was immediate:

"Then Moses lifted up his hand and struck the rock twice with his rod; and water came forth abundantly, and the congregation and their beasts drank. But the LORD said to Moses and Aaron, 'Because you have not believed Me, to treat Me as holy in the sight of the sons of Israel, therefore you shall not bring this assembly into the land which I have given them.'" (Numbers 20:11-12)

Holiness is a person. Our disobedience to His revealed will represents a personal affront to the God Whose Presence and holiness are "a consuming fire."

We could offer numerous illustrations of this principle of *"Be separate, or be consumed."* For example, in Leviticus Chapter 22 we read about how God in His holiness set aside certain things (such as offerings) for His purposes. And in Leviticus 23 we discover how God in His holiness set aside certain days as required feast days. But through all of these examples, and more which we could offer from the Old Testament, the guiding principle was the same. God is holy, and we must treat Him as holy by obedience in all that we say and do.

Throughout the Old Testament, God's holiness was NOT something to be trifled with or taken lightly. Familiarity with God was NOT something widely known or experienced among OT saints. The requirements of such separations were VERY stringent and unforgiving, and the punishment for violators who failed to treat Him as holy - especially in the eyes of the people - was swift and harsh. Just ask Nadab and Abihu.

The Inextinguishable Blaze

Nadab, Abihu And The Price of Holiness

"Now Nadab and Abihu, the sons of Aaron, took their respective firepans, and after putting fire in them, placed incense on it and offered strange fire before the LORD, which He had not commanded them. And fire came out from the presence of the LORD and consumed them, and they died before the LORD. Then Moses said to Aaron, 'It is what the LORD spoke, saying, 'By those who come near Me I will be treated as holy, And before all the people I will be honored.' So Aaron, therefore, kept silent." (Leviticus 10:1-3)

According to Scripture, on the day of Atonement, the High Priest was to enter into the Holy of Holies and sprinkle blood on the Mercy Seat atop the Ark of the Covenant between the covering Cherubim, where the Presence of God dwelt (See Leviticus 16). He was to do this in atonement for the sins of the people in an act that foreshadowed the sacrificial death and atonement of a future Saviour. According to tradition, before the High Priest entered the Holy of Holies his fellow priests would tie a rope around his ankle so that should the Holy One of Israel strike him down in the Holy of Holies the priests could retrieve his body. That's the tradition. Nadab and Abihu are the reality which makes the tradition believable.

Nadab and Abihu were sons born to Aaron while the people of God were still in Egypt (Exodus 6:3). They made their first public appearance as adults when God invited and called them along with Moses, Aaron and the 70 elders of Israel to have fellowship with Him on Mount Sinai in Exodus 24:1ff. Later, in Exodus 28, God appointed them to serve as priests to minister before Him. Nothing more is said about them until the episode which we read about in Leviticus Chapter 10.

According to bits and pieces of information we can glean

Be Separate, Or Be Consumed

from Leviticus 10 and 16, here is what appears to have happened. Nadab and Abihu were indeed priests appointed to minister before the Lord. Their assigned responsibilities involved offering incense in the Tent of Meeting where Priests could go, but the people could not. But one day the two of them had a bit too much to drink (see 10:8-10) and decided that they could, should and would move beyond their assigned responsibilities by entering and offering incense in the Holy of Holies, which contained the Ark of the Covenant and was separated by a veil from the rest of the Tent of Meeting. By doing this Nadab and Abihu did two things. First, they violated the very strict and specific boundaries of separation which the Law required. Only the High Priest could enter the Holy of Holies, and then only on the Day of Atonement. But secondly, and this really speaks to the heart of the issue, Nadab and Abihu failed to treat God as holy, and thereby failed to honor Him before others. And that was fatal. *"And fire came out from the presence of the LORD and consumed them."* Here we have the summation of the purpose behind all of the Old Testament rules, ordinances and laws regarding holiness and separation. They existed to teach God's people how to treat God as holy. *"Be separate, or be consumed."* Failure to keep them - any of them - represented a personal failure to treat and honor God as holy before others. And that was a failure which could not be tolerated, whether by them, by Moses, by Aaron or by anyone else. Then or now.

In an epilogue to this episode, it is noteworthy that Nadab and Abihu weren't stoned to death, shot with arrows or swallowed up by the ground opening up beneath them (as with

"Holiness is personal, not legal. God takes the violation of His holiness personally."

Korah and Dathan in Numbers 16:1-33). No, they were

The Inextinguishable Blaze

personally consumed by fire which came directly from the very Presence of the God Whose holiness is "a consuming fire." Holiness is personal, not legal. God takes the violation of His holiness personally. *"Be separate, or be consumed."*

The Inextinguishable Blaze

"I believe God has to accomplish a work in us before we can lay claim to any covenant promise. What is this precedent work upon which all others depend? Jeremiah tells us: 'I will put My fear in their hearts so that they will not depart from Me' (Jeremiah 32:40). God's precedent work of the covenant is to put His fear into our hearts by the work of the Holy Spirit."[43]

It is time for the Church of our generation to embrace the fire of God's holiness and the genuine fear of God it brings. We as a Church have lost our fear of God. The fire of God's Presence and holiness can and will restore that fear. The question becomes, *"Is that what we want?"* It is most certainly what we need in this hour. God is not looking for a new generation of Christian "lawyers" - experts on the pseudo-holiness of legalism and rule keeping. He is looking to raise up a generation of Christian firebrands, *"children of the burning heart"* whose lives are flaming embers, carriers of "the Inextinguishable Blaze." Are you one of them?

The world of our generation is perishing because it has yet to see the fire and the power of a genuinely holy Church. Are you prepared to show it to them?

---

[43]David Wilkerson, *"The Piercing Arrows of Holy Truth,"* Friday, October 21, 2011, posted online at http://www.worldchallenge.org/

Chapter 7

Once Upon A Mountain

"And all the people perceived the thunder and the lightning flashes and the sound of the trumpet and the mountain smoking; and when the people saw it, they trembled and stood at a distance. Then they said to Moses, 'Speak to us yourself and we will listen; but let not God speak to us, lest we die.' And Moses said to the people, 'Do not be afraid; for God has come in order to test you, and in order that the fear of Him may remain with you, so that you may not sin.'" (Exodus 20:18-20)

The consuming fire of God's holiness is something that the people of Israel discovered very early in their relationship with God. Three months after leaving Egypt, the people of Israel stood at the foot of Mt. Sinai where they were soon introduced to both holiness and fear.

A quick overview might be helpful at this point. The Book of Exodus divides into two basic sections. The first section (Chapters 1-18) deals with the events of the Exodus, while the second section (Chapters 19-40) deals with the Covenant at Mt. Sinai. All of the events recorded in the second section take place either upon or at the foot of Mt. Sinai.

Chapter 19 records the arrival of the people at Mt. Sinai where God explains to them why they are there: to become His unique possession, *"a kingdom of priests and a holy nation."* (Exodus 19:6). In order to meet with God and enter into this covenant relationship, two full days of preparation are necessary. The people must wash their garments, abstain from sexual activity and be instructed in the limits or boundaries of the mountain; where they can approach

The Inextinguishable Blaze

without touching it and violating God's holiness.[44]

Then, on the third day, it happened. The God whose presence and whose holiness are "a consuming fire" came down upon the mountain, *"Now Mount Sinai was all in smoke because the LORD descended upon it in fire; and its smoke ascended like the smoke of a furnace, and the whole mountain quaked violently. When the sound of the trumpet grew louder and louder, Moses spoke and God answered him with thunder. And the LORD came down on Mount Sinai, to the top of the mountain"* .(Exodus 19:18-20) There was fire, trumpet blasts, earthquakes and even the very voice of God Himself audibly speaking the ten commandments in the hearing of all the people (Exodus 20:1-17). There was also fear among the people standing at the foot of the mountain in the Presence of this holy God Who was *"a consuming fire"* upon the mountain.

And it was at this point, as we read from Exodus 20:18-20 (see above), that Moses told the people of Israel something that needs repeating today and which I will paraphrase here: *"Don't be afraid to embrace the fear of God. It will keep you from sinning."* And that deserves some exploration.

Holiness And The Fear of God

"The fear of the Lord is the beginning of wisdom" (Psalm 111:10; Proverbs 1:7 & 9:10)

---

[44]While this requirement of abstinence might seem unusual at first glance, it is consistent with the principle of sexual activity and abstinence between husband and wife which Paul gives in 1 Corinthians 7:5 - namely, abstinence *"by agreement for a time that you may devote yourselves to prayer."* When understood from this perspective it was a reasonable requirement for a season of prayer and preparation for meeting with God.

Once Upon A Mountain

"When men no longer fear God, they transgress His laws without hesitation. The fear of consequences is no deterrent when the fear of God is gone." [45]

I have always thought it noteworthy that the FEAR of the Lord is the beginning of wisdom; NOT His love. Three times in Scripture we are told that *"the fear of the Lord is the beginning of wisdom."* But not once does Scripture ever tell us that the Love of God is the beginning of wisdom. This may seem counter-intuitive to a generation of Christians who have come to focus almost exclusively on God's love. But the biblical reality is that fear teaches us things that love never will. Fear shatters our comfort zones and causes our hearts to tremble, *"so that all the people who were in the camp trembled."* (Exodus 19:16) The trembling heart is a teachable heart. And as Moses instructed the people of God at Mt. Sinai, one of the first things the fear of God will teach us is **not** to sin.

> *"I have always thought it noteworthy that the FEAR of the Lord is the beginning of wisdom; NOT His love."*

Most Scriptural teaching on the topic of fear centers around God instructing His people not to fear people, events or circumstances. Over 50 times in Scripture God admonishes and encourages people with the words *"Do not fear"* with respect to people or events or circumstances. But Scripture recognizes and even commands another type of fear, namely, the "fear of God." Some 25 times the Scriptures specifically tell people to "fear the Lord." At the end of his search for wisdom the Preacher of Ecclesiastes (Solomon)

---

[45]Tozer, *The Knowledge of the Holy*, page 77.

The Inextinguishable Blaze

declared, *"Now all has been heard; here is the conclusion of the matter: Fear God and keep his commandments, for this is the whole duty of man"* (Ecclesiastes 12:13). Solomon had discovered what his father, David, had understood and taught when he wrote under the inspiration of the Holy Spirit, *"The fear of the Lord is clean . . ."* (Psalm 19:9).

We live today in a generation of contemporary believers who have lost any genuine sense of "the fear of God," and as a result they have lost their fear

> *"The trembling heart is a teachable heart."*

of sinning against a holy God Who regards all sin as a personal affront to His holiness. I would attribute this loss to at least three things. I would begin by assigning blame to ill-informed bible teachers who have offered a great deal of bad teaching, including lukewarm assurances that the "fear of God" which Scripture encourages is really some innocuous, non-threatening concept called "reverential awe." The genuine "fear of God" which gripped the Israelites standing at the foot of Mt. Sinai and which caused them to "tremble" was something quite different from the vaguely defined "reverential awe" promoted by most Bible teachers and preachers today.[46] Next, I would attribute our loss of "the fear of God" to our lack of understanding concerning God's holiness in all of its fullness. Finally, I would attribute our loss of "the fear of God" to the absence of God's genuine Presence in most of what the contemporary church does today. I have lost track of the number of church gatherings I have been in where lively worship music was mistaken for

---

[46]This bad teaching is often aided by people quoting the King James rendering of 2 Timothy 1:7, *"For God hath not given us the spirit of fear."* But the Greek word translated "fear" by the King James is actually the Greek word for "timidity" (*deilia*), NOT the Greek word for "fear" (*phobos*).

Once Upon A Mountain

God's Presence. The goal of the average evangelical church in America is simple: to see to it that those who attend the performance leave having had "a positive religious experience." Everything in the service, from the music to the announcements to the skit to the message, is geared toward that end. And it is that "positive religious experience" that everyone agrees to refer to as "the Presence of God." We can only wonder what contemporary church attenders would have done and how they would have responded at the foot of Mt. Sinai.

The Mountain And The Church

"For you have not come to a mountain that may be touched and to a blazing fire, and to darkness and gloom and whirlwind, and to the blast of a trumpet and the sound of words which sound was such that those who heard begged that no further word should be spoken to them. For they could not bear the command, 'IF EVEN A BEAST TOUCHES THE MOUNTAIN, IT WILL BE STONED.' And so terrible was the sight, that Moses said, 'I AM FULL OF FEAR and trembling' . . . . Therefore, since we receive a kingdom which cannot be shaken, let us show gratitude, by which we may offer to God an acceptable service with reverence and awe; for our God is a consuming fire." (Hebrews 12:18-29)

The New Testament writer of the letter to the Hebrews was very familiar with the events of Exodus 19-20 at the foot of Mt. Sinai. He refers to them in detail in Hebrews Chapter 12, where he explains the relationship between what God did on Mt. Sinai and what He has now done in the Church.

The theme of Hebrews is the surpassing greatness and superiority of Christ along with the superiority of what God has done in the Church over what He did at Mt. Sinai. The writer goes into detail to describe the surpassing greatness

The Inextinguishable Blaze

of the salvation which we have been offered in Christ, and the terrible consequences if we should neglect or refuse it. The writer makes an argument which connects the Old Testament to the New Testament.

He begins his argument by explaining the greatness of the fear which the children of Israel experienced as they stood at the foot of Mt. Sinai in the Presence of God. In verse 21 he describes Moses as saying, *"I am full of fear and trembling."* Most English translators have muted this verse. The literal rendering of the Greek text here is a bit more intense. *"I am terrified out of my wits,"* would be a more honest translation of the text. As we observed earlier, there is no such thing as "lukewarm fire." It is in the same category as "reverential awe."

The author then emphasizes the surpassing greatness and superiority of what we have received as participants in the Church over what the Israelites received at Mt. Sinai. They experienced a shaking mountain and received a spoken word. We have received an unshakable Kingdom and the Word Incarnate.

Moving his argument forward the writer admonishes his readers that, in light of the surpassing greatness of the Kingdom we have received over what the Israelites received at Mt. Sinai, our service of worship should be characterized not only by gratitude on our part, but by both a reverent humility and a godly fear.

Finally, the author makes his point and connects the Old Testament with the New. God hasn't changed. The God Whose Holy Presence was "a consuming fire" upon Mt. Sinai is the same God Whose Holy Presence is now a consuming fire in the Church. ***Our God is STILL "a consuming fire."***

Once Upon A Mountain

When The "Consuming Fire" Visits A Church

Reading the biblical account of Israel's experience with the consuming fire of God's holiness at Mt. Sinai and its counterpart in the Church of God is instructive and challenging. But as we reflect on it we cannot help but ask ourselves what it might look like when the consuming fire of God's holiness and presence manifests in the midst of God's people today. Fortunately, we do not need to look very far for an answer.

In 1904 a worldwide spiritual outpouring began in the tiny country of Wales. Beginning as a burning coal fresh from God's altar under the ministry of a Welsh pastor named Joseph Jenkins in February of 1904, it soon became a spreading flame, igniting a fire in the itinerant ministry of a Welsh evangelist named Seth Joshua. Under his preaching in September of 1904 the fire burst into an uncontrollable wildfire led and fanned by a 26 year old former coal miner and first-year Bible school student named Evan Roberts who was quickly consumed by"the Inextinguishable Blaze." From Wales the fire spread east, west, north and south, making a brief-but-memorable stop at an abandoned livery stable turned church on Azusa Street in Los Angeles in 1906. Finally, it burned its way to Korea where it broke out among Presbyterian Missionaries meeting with their congregations for a week of Bible school during the first week of January, 1907.

To this day, Presbyterian missionaries still refer to the events of that week. The incredible growth of the modern evangelical church in Korea has its roots in God's visitation among His people during that week in January of 1907. Those events are best described by one of the missionaries who was there and was both a witness and a participant. What follows is William Newton Blair's account of that

The Inextinguishable Blaze

Tuesday night in January of 1907 when our God Whose Presence and holiness are "a consuming fire" came down and visited His people.

I wish to describe that Tuesday night meeting in my own words because part of what happened concerned me personally. We were aware that bad feeling existed between several of our church officers, especially between a Mr. Kang and a Mr. Kim. Mr. Kang confessed his hatred for Mr. Kim on Monday night, but Mr. Kim was silent. At our noon prayer-meeting Tuesday several of us agreed to pray for Mr. Kim. I was especially interested because Mr. Kang was my assistant in the North Pyengyang Church and Mr. Kim, an elder in the Central Church and one of the officers in the Young Men's Association of which I was chairman. As the meeting progressed, I could see Mr. Kim sitting with the elders back of the pulpit with his head down. Bowing where I sat I asked God to help him and looking up I saw him coming forward

Holding to the pulpit he made his confession. 'I have been guilty of fighting against God. An elder in the church, I have been guilty of hating not only Kang You-moon, but Pang Moksa.' Pang Moksa was my Korean name. I never had a greater surprise in my life. To think that this man, my associate in the Men's Association, had been hating me without my knowing it. It seems that I had said something to him one day in the hurry of managing a school field day exercise which had given offense, and he had not been able to forgive me.

Turning to me he said, 'Can you forgive me? Can you pray for me?' I stood up and began to pray, 'Aba-ge, Aba-ge,' 'Father, Father,' and got no further. It seemed as if the roof was lifted from the building and the Spirit of God came down in a mighty avalanche of power upon us. I fell at Kim's side

Once Upon A Mountain

and wept and prayed as I had never prayed before. My last glimpse of the audience is photographed indelibly on my brain. Some threw themselves full length on the floor, hundreds stood with arms outstretched towards heaven. Every man forgot every other. Each was face to face with God. I can hear yet that fearful sound of hundreds of men pleading with God for mercy.

As soon as we were able, we missionaries gathered at the platform and consulted. 'What shall we do? If we let them go on this way some will go crazy.' Yet we dared not interfere. We had prayed to God for an outpouring of His Holy Spirit upon the people and it had come. Separating, we went down and tried to comfort the most distressed, pulling the agonized men to the floor and saying, 'Never mind, brother, if you have sinned God will forgive you. Wait and an opportunity will be given to speak.'

Finally Dr. Lee started a hymn and quiet was restored during the singing. Then began a meeting the like of which I had never seen before, nor wish to see again unless in God's sight it is absolutely necessary. Every sin a human being can commit was publicly confessed that night. Pale and trembling with emotion, in agony of mind and body, guilty souls standing in the white light of that judgment, saw themselves as God saw them. Their sins rose up in all their vileness 'till shame and grief and self-loathing took complete possession. Pride was driven out; the face of man forgotten. Looking up to heaven, to Jesus whom they had betrayed, they smote themselves and cried out with bitter wailing, 'Lord, Lord, cast us not away forever.' Everything else was forgotten; nothing else mattered. The scorn of men, the penalty of the law, even death itself seemed of small consequence if only God forgave. We may have our theories of the desirability or undesirability of public confession of sin. I have had mine, but I know now that when the Spirit of God falls upon guilty

The Inextinguishable Blaze

souls there will be confession and no power on earth can stop it." [47]

Welcome to the Church at the foot of Mt. Sinai.

The Inextinguishable Blaze

It is time for the Church to repent and return to the foot of Mt. Sinai. NOT a return to a law of types and shadows which has been fulfilled in Christ, but a recovery the Presence and holiness of our God Who is "a consuming fire" in the midst of His people. The fire of God's holiness in the midst of His Church will accomplish in our lives corporately and individually what the law never could - inward transformation.

And one of the first steps is for us to discard our religious veils and to admit to ourselves and to God that we no longer carry *"the Inextinguishable Blaze"* of His Presence on our faces or in our lives. It is time for us to admit what a skeptical watching world already knows: We have substituted a religious veil for the fire.

And that is where we need to go next.

---

[47] *"The Korean Pentecost,"* excerpted from **Gold In Korea**, by William Newton Blair. Available through the Central Distributing Department of the Presbyterian Church (USA). 3rd edition (1957)

Chapter 8

Holiness And The Veil

"And it came about when Moses was coming down from Mount Sinai (and the two tablets of the testimony were in Moses' hand as he was coming down from the mountain), that Moses did not know that the skin of his face shone because of his speaking with Him. So when Aaron and all the sons of Israel saw Moses, behold, the skin of his face shone, and they were afraid to come near him. Then Moses called to them, and Aaron and all the rulers in the congregation returned to him; and Moses spoke to them. And afterward all the sons of Israel came near, and he commanded them to do everything that the Lord had spoken to him on Mount Sinai. When Moses had finished speaking with them, he put a veil over his face. But whenever Moses went in before the Lord to speak with Him, he would take off the veil until he came out; and whenever he came out and spoke to the sons of Israel what he had been commanded, the sons of Israel would see the face of Moses, that the skin of Moses' face shone. So Moses would replace the veil over his face until he went in to speak with Him. (Exodus 34:29-35)

Welcome back to the foot of Mt. Sinai and to those formative events which would shape the people of God for a millennium and provide the basis for much New Testament teaching. The last half of the book of Exodus contains numerous stories or "anecdotes" which capture God's dealings among His people at this critical moment. This particular passage relates one of the events surrounding Moses' second sojourn on Mt. Sinai to receive the Ten Commandments written on stone. The first sojourn had ended badly with Moses destroying the original tablets out of anger over the incident of the golden calf (See Exodus 32). This trip was somewhat different from the first one. Just prior to God commanding him to ascend the mountain for the

The Inextinguishable Blaze

second time, Moses had made a bold request of God: *"Then Moses said, 'I pray Thee, show me Thy glory!'"* (Exodus 33:18).

It is a spiritual truth that every man (or woman) has as much of God as he or she truly desires to have. Or as A. W. Tozer observed, *"Every man is as holy as he really wants to be."*[48] I have noticed over the years of my Christian experience that what people say they want in their walk with God and what they are actually willing to pursue are often quite different. Many people will opine about their desire for a more intimate walk with God, but when confronted with the price of pursuing and receiving more from God they shrink away. This was unfortunately true of many (if not most) of God's people encamped at the foot of Mt. Sinai. Fresh from their miraculous deliverance on the shore of the Red Sea, the people were enthusiastic in their desire to obey and pursue God. Listen to their declaration to Moses:

> *"It is a spiritual truth that every man (or woman) has as much of God as he or she truly desires to have."*

"So Moses came and called the elders of the people, and set before them all these words which the LORD had commanded him. And all the people answered together and said, 'All that the LORD has spoken we will do!' And Moses brought back the words of the people to the LORD." (Exodus 19:7-8)

But their enthusiasm was short-lived. Soon, (three days later) they were confronted with the reality of God's Presence in

---

[48]A. W. Tozer, *"How to Make Spiritual Progress"* in **Man - The Dwelling Place of God** (Fig Books 2012 Edition), page 30.

Holiness And The Veil

power and in holiness upon the mountain. God manifested Himself, the people responded and we have the account:

"And all the people perceived the thunder and the lightning flashes and the sound of the trumpet and the mountain smoking; and when the people saw it, they trembled and stood at a distance. Then they said to Moses, 'Speak to us yourself and we will listen; but let not God speak to us, lest we die.' And Moses said to the people, 'Do not be afraid; for God has come in order to test you, and in order that the fear of Him may remain with you, so that you may not sin.' So the people stood at a distance, while Moses approached the thick cloud where God was." (Exodus 20:18-21)

It is an undeniable spiritual reality that God tests the hearts of believers,[49] and this was one of those spiritual tests. The Hebrew word rendered "test" in Exodus 20:20 is the same word used in Genesis 22:1 where we are told that *"God tested Abraham"* in the matter of

> *"God asks us questions and tests our heart in order to reveal to us what He already knows: whether or not we are genuinely willing to trust Him."*

sacrificing his son, Isaac. Prior to their arrival at Mt. Sinai God had already tested the people of Israel regarding their willingness to trust Him to provide water (See Exodus 15:25) and food (See Exodus 16:4).

The purpose of God's spiritual tests is not to elicit information that He doesn't already have. God doesn't ask questions because He is short on information. God asks us questions

---

[49]See Genesis 22:1; Exodus 15:25 & 16:4; Deuteronomy 8:16; Judges 2:22 & 3:1; Psalm 11:4; Jeremiah 17:10 & 20:12: Zechariah 13:9

The Inextinguishable Blaze

and tests our heart in order to reveal to us what He already knows: whether or not we are genuinely willing to trust Him. And to reveal for all to see whether or not we are willing to pay the price for pursuing genuine holiness, fear, repentance and intimacy with Him.

The result of this test at the foot of Mt. Sinai is well summarized by verse 21 of chapter 20: *"So the people stood at a distance, while Moses approached the thick cloud where God was."* This test revealed two things. On the one hand, it revealed the limits of Israel's willingness to pursue God. They simply were not willing to pay the price of drawing any closer to this God Whose presence and holiness were "a consuming fire" upon the mountain. We can only speculate if this self-imposed limitation on growing closer to God played any role in the episode of the golden calf which would unfold in the next forty days while Moses was on the mountain receiving the tablets of the law. On the other hand, this test revealed the genuine heart-felt desire of Moses to press on with God, *"Moses approached the thick cloud where God was."* In Psalm 103 the Psalmist gives us a one-sentence summary and epilogue concerning this difference between the relationship Moses had with God, and the relationship that of the people of Israel had with God: *"He made known His ways to Moses, His acts to the sons of Israel."* (Psalm 103:7)

The implication of this verse (even in the Hebrew) is that Moses achieved an intimacy with God that the people never did. To Moses, God chose to make known His "ways." But all that the people ever really knew of God was His "acts" - water from a rock, manna in the morning, quail in the evening, and a glory cloud over the tabernacle. Moses met with God like a friend, learned the heart of the God of Holiness and came to understand why He did what He did. The people chose to stand at a distance, satisfied with "signs

Holiness And The Veil

and wonders" but never really entering into intimacy with God. There is a difference between knowing God's hand and knowing his heart. To know God in His "acts" of signs and wonders is to know His hand. To Know God's "ways" is to discover His heart and to carry *"the Inextinguishable Blaze"* of His holiness and His Presence.

Fire On The Face

Moses' request that God would *"show me Thy glory"* represented a heart-felt desire to know more of God's Presence (Exodus 33:14-15). So, on this second encounter on the mountain, God allowed Moses to stand in His Presence and to experience His glory:

"And the LORD descended in the cloud and stood there with him as he called upon the name of the LORD. Then the LORD passed by in front of him and proclaimed, 'The LORD, the LORD God, compassionate and gracious, slow to anger, and abounding in loving-kindness and truth; who keeps loving-kindness for thousands, who forgives iniquity, transgression and sin; yet He will by no means leave the guilty unpunished, visiting the iniquity of fathers on the children and on the grandchildren to the third and fourth generations.' And Moses made haste to bow low toward the earth and worship." (34:5-8)

God allowed Moses to stand in His undimmed presence. This particular encounter with God had a different effect from previous encounters. Moses was in the habit of meeting regularly with God, (Exodus 33:11, *"Thus the LORD used to speak to Moses face to face, just as a man speaks to his friend"*). But this encounter was different, and such encounters with the God Whose holiness and presence is "a consuming fire" can produce unpredictable effects on people. This time the revelation of God's glory rubbed off on Moses.

The Inextinguishable Blaze

The unanticipated effect of experiencing God's unmuted and undimmed glory was that the skin of his face shone with God's glory. In the words of the song-writer, *"His face was set on fire, as the God of glory shone."* The fire and the glory of God's Presence lingered on the face of Moses.

Moses' encounter with God had an effect on those around him that was immediate and profound, *"they were afraid to come near him."* People who know little of God's glory, or the fire of

"There is something in our nature that quickly turns an accommodation-to-weakness into a mis-applied spiritual principle."

His Presence, are often frightened by people whose faces glow from the glory of God' Presence and whose clothes still carry the smell of holy fire. Moses accommodated their fear by wearing a veil to cover his face and to hide the glow of God's glory.

There is something in our nature that quickly turns an accommodation-to-weakness into a mis-applied spiritual principle. In this situation such a mis-applied spiritual principle might sound like this: *"Holy people wear veils; so, if you want people to think you are holy, you should wear a veil."* This, in a genuine sense, is what happened to Moses. How do we know? Because Scripture tells us. Reflecting on this incident with Moses and the veil, the Apostle Paul comments on Moses' accommodation. Listen carefully to what Paul says:

"Having therefore such a hope, we use great boldness in our speech, and are not as Moses, who used to put a veil over his face that the sons of Israel might not look intently at the end of what was fading away." (2 Corinthians 3:12-13)

Holiness And The Veil

Paul's observation and implication are clear. Moses understood the fading nature of God's glory beneath the veil, but he continued to wear the veil beyond what was necessary because he didn't want the people of Israel to see that the glory was fading away.

Lessons In Holiness, Veils And The Pursuit of God

The experiences of God's people at the foot of Mt. Sinai, including Moses and the veil, can teach us some important spiritual truths, if we will just take the time to listen, to reflect and to learn.

Holiness is the Presence, the fire and the glow; not the veil. God's Presence and holiness are a fire, not a formula. A Person, not a program. It is the fire of God's holiness, not a set of laws, rules and regulations, which produces genuine holiness in us. But genuine fire is scary stuff. Moses and the people of God

> *"Holiness is His Presence, the fire and the glow, not the veil."*

discovered this truth at Mt. Sinai. Moses embraced it and cried out for more. The people, for the most part, were frightened by it and cried out to be spared any more. *"Then they said to Moses, 'Speak to us yourself and we will listen; but let not God speak to us, lest we die.'"* (Exodus 20:19) Holiness is a relationship and a fire, not a set of rules or laws or even mis-applied spiritual principles springing from God's accommodations to our weaknesses. Holiness is His Presence, the fire and the glow, not the veil. One of the spiritual truths from the mountain is that it is always easier (or at least safer) to follow a set of rules than it is to pursue the fire of holiness and to stand in His Presence. The people chose the rules. Moses chose the fire. There is a lesson for

The Inextinguishable Blaze

all of us in there somewhere.

Mistaking the veil for the fire. Many of the churches and denominations which litter the church landscape today were born out of the fires of a genuine encounter with God. Methodism was born from the fires of the Evangelical Awakening in England. The Salvation Army was born from the fires of the Second Evangelical Awakening in England during the mid-1800s. Most Pentecostal denominations, such as the Assemblies of God, were born out of the fires of the 1904-1907 worldwide awakening that began in Wales. The Calvary Chapel denomination along with The Vineyard Association of Churches were both born out of the fires of the Jesus Movement. We could cite other examples but these are enough to make our point.

The fires of genuine spiritual awakening produce genuine holiness, the fear of God, repentance, renewed intimacy with God. But they eventually produce something else. Religious veils. Rules for religious behavior designed to perpetuate the appearance of God's Presence in the midst of His people long after the glory has departed.

Like Moses among the people of Israel, the Church in America and the West today has held tightly to the veils of previous seasons of Divine visitation. But it has long since lost the Presence. Far too much of what we do, from our programs to our vocabulary, has become little more than a veil in search of a fire. We boldly claim to serve "hot, fresh baked bread." But upon close inspection people discover that our ovens are cold and the bread is little more than a left-over that has been warmed up in a microwave. Once upon a time in our experiences with God our faces may have burned and glowed with His Presence, but no more. Somewhere in the process we kept the veil but lost the Presence. We have made peace with keeping the religious rules, but in the

Holiness And The Veil

process we have lost the fire of God's holiness and Presence. While most of our Postmodern culture may be spiritually blind and clueless in any genuine biblical terms, it has been perceptive enough to notice the absence of any genuine fire, either in our lives or in the Church.

The Inextinguishable Blaze

"Because you say, 'I am rich, and have become wealthy, and have need of nothing,' and you do not know that you are wretched and miserable and poor and blind and naked" (Revelation 3:17)

Lukewarm believers frequently hide behind the veil of religious activities designed to mask their true spiritual condition and to convince themselves and others that they are *"rich, wealthy and in need of nothing"* when in reality they are spiritually *"miserable, poor, blind and naked."* Like the Church of Laodicea the Church in America and the West is the most affluent and "in-need-of-nothing" Church in history when it comes to programs, activities and money. But the truth is that all of our programs, activities and money represent little more than a religious veil to hide our spiritual poverty; the conspicuous absence of the consuming fire of God's Presence and holiness in our midst. And it has been absent for so long that we don't even miss it and have come to regard the situation as "normal."

It is time for the Church of our generation to repent of our religious veils and to seek *"the Inextinguishable Blaze"* of God's Presence and holiness. The world of our generation is perishing because it has yet to see the fire and the power of a genuinely holy Church. Are you prepared to show it to them, or are you still hiding behind a religious veil?

The Inextinguishable Blaze

Chapter 9

Samson: Holiness, Character And Gifting

"And Samson said, 'Let me die with the Philistines.' Then he bowed with all his strength, and the house fell upon the lords and upon all the people who were in it. So the dead whom he killed at his death were more than those whom he had killed during his life." (Judges 16:30)

"Strive for peace with everyone, and for the holiness without which no one will see the Lord." (Hebrews 12:14)

Earlier we discovered that, for the average Israelite, Old Testament holiness emphasized outward physical separation. As we saw, the rules of separation were fixed and inflexible, and the punishment for breaching them was swift and harsh (as Nadab and Abihu discovered). The separations of God's holiness were not open to negotiation. One couldn't simply conclude after prayer one morning that God was calling him or her "into the ministry" as a priest. If you weren't a Levite and a son of Aaron, that simply wasn't an option. So, besides obeying all of the rules of separation, how could the average Israelite express his or her desire for greater holiness and for greater personal devotion to God? Enter the Law of the Nazirite.

The Law of the Nazirite is described in detail in Numbers 6. A Nazirite was an individual (either man or woman) who entered into *"a special vow . . . . to separate himself to the LORD"* (Numbers 6:2). The Nazirite vow of separation was normally for a limited period of time and involved three commitments which were to last for the period of his (or her) separation. **First,** the Nazirite vow involved a personal commitment to separate oneself from wine or strong drink or anything made of grapes, *"he shall separate himself from wine and strong drink. He shall drink no vinegar made from*

The Inextinguishable Blaze

wine or strong drink and shall not drink any juice of grapes or eat grapes, fresh or dried. All the days of his separation he shall eat nothing that is produced by the grapevine, not even the seeds or the skins" (Numbers 6:3-4).

Second, it involved a personal commitment not to cut one's hair, *"All the days of his vow of separation, no razor shall touch his head. Until the time is completed for which he separates himself to the LORD, he shall be holy. He shall let the locks of hair of his head grow long"* (Numbers 6:5). This commitment effectively created a public declaration for all to see that this person was under the Nazirite vow of separation and holiness.

Third, the Nazirite vow involved a personal commitment not to go near a dead body, any dead body, including that of a family member (Numbers 6:6). The requirements were strict. The violation of any one of these commitments constituted a breach of the vow and required that the individual shave his head, offer appropriate sacrifices and start his vow over from the beginning, *"the previous period shall be void, because his separation was defiled"* (Numbers 6:12).

The separation of the Nazirites offered a public testimony to the challenge of being a holy people and sent a clear message: Personal holiness requires a significant degree of personal discipline on our part. The Scriptures record three lifelong Nazirites-from-birth: Samuel, Samson and John the Baptist. We want to look at the life of one of them: Samson.

Samson The Nazirite

Samson was the 12th and last Judge of ancient Israel. His parents were from the small tribe of Dan. His life was auspicious from the beginning. An angel appeared to his parents and announced that they would have a son who

Samson: Holiness, Character And Gifting

would be a Nazirite from His birth. Prior to his appearance as an adult the only thing we are told about Samson is that *"the young man grew, and the LORD blessed him"* (Judges 13:36). Fortunately for us, Samson's life conveniently divides into three sections which we will briefly examine.

Samson's Birth, which was supernaturally foretold (Judges 13). Samson's birth and ministry were supernaturally foretold. But that calling was first and foremost a calling to holiness and separation as a Nazirite, *"Until the time is completed for which he separates himself to the LORD, he shall be holy"* (Numbers 6:5). There is a lesson here that we must not miss. Supernatural calling does not guarantee either personal holiness or spiritual success. Nor does it give us a special "pass" when it comes to obedience. It simply makes us accountable to the promise on our lives.

Samson's deliverance of Israel from the Philistines, which was spiritually powerful (Judges 14:1-15:20). This section represents the "high water mark" of Samson's ministry. In the five incidents recorded during this time, three of those five are characterized by the phrase *"The Spirit of the Lord rushed upon Him"* (see 14:6, 19, 15:14). But it was during this same time of apparent success, when he confounded the Philistines and killed just over 1,000 men, that the flaws of Samson's character began to manifest themselves.

The first issue arose in the incident of the lion, *"Then Samson went down with his father and mother to Timnah, and they came to the vineyards of Timnah. And behold, a young lion came toward him roaring. Then the Spirit of the LORD rushed upon him, and although he had nothing in his hand, he tore the lion in pieces as one tears a young goat"* (Judges 14:5-6). Under the power of the Holy Spirit, Samson killed a charging lion with his bare hands. No problem, and God was

The Inextinguishable Blaze

in it. The problem arose with what happened next:

"After some days he returned to take her. And he turned aside to see the carcass of the lion, and behold, there was a swarm of bees in the body of the lion, and honey. He scraped it out into his hands and went on, eating as he went. And he came to his father and mother and gave some to them, and they ate. But he did not tell them that he had scraped the honey from the carcass of the lion." (Judges 14:8-9)

The Law of the Nazirite was clear. Contact with a dead body, any dead body, was a violation of the Nazirite vow. It meant immediate termination of the vow. The individual must shave his head and offer appropriate sacrifices and start the period of his vow over from the beginning (Numbers 6:9-12). If there could be such a thing as an "over the top" violation of his vow, scraping honey from the carcass of a dead lion would be it. Samson's failure to inform his mother and father regarding the source of the honey strongly suggests that he understood what he had done. They, too, would have known that Samson had knowingly broken his Nazirite vow. And now he had lied about it.

A second issue arose with the marriage feast which Samson held in preparation for marrying a Philistine woman. The Scriptures tell us that the marriage was *"from the LORD, for he was seeking an opportunity against the Philistines."* (Judges 14:4) But the wedding feast itself presented a different problem. The Hebrew word translated "feast" in verse 10 ("*mishteh*") specifically refers to a feast involving the consumption of alcohol. To put it in contemporary terms, Samson threw a seven-day long "kegger." For the writer of Judges to use this term can only be understood as a commentary on the obvious - by his actions Samson violated his Nazirite vow by consuming alcohol.

Samson: Holiness, Character And Gifting

A third problem arose when Samson used *"the fresh jawbone of a donkey"* to kill a thousand Philistines in Judges 15:15: *"When he came to Lehi, the Philistines came shouting to meet him. Then the Spirit of the LORD rushed upon him, and the ropes that were on his arms became as flax that has caught fire, and his bonds melted off his hands. And he found a fresh jawbone of a donkey, and put out his hand and took it, and with it he struck 1,000 men."* (Judges 15:14-15)

The writer of Judges makes several important points in this story. He begins by making it clear that "the Spirit of the Lord" enabled Samson to break the ropes which were holding him. But the writer goes on to tell us that Samson found "a fresh jawbone" of a donkey. The clear implication here is that this was the jawbone of a recently dead carcass (another "dead body"). The writer then goes out of his way to tells us that Samson *"put out his hand and took it."* The writer wants us to understand that Samson knowingly "put out his hand" and violated his Nazirite vow. He could have looked for a different weapon, or he could have fought bare-handed (as he had done with the lion), or he could have run away. But he didn't. He made a choice which was a direct and willful violation of his calling and his vow to holiness and separation. We shouldn't kid ourselves or excuse Samson at this point. God took note of this moment. The incident with the jawbone would be the last time that *"the Spirit of the Lord"* would ever come upon Samson. God's patience had run out with His wayward Nazirite.

Samson's personal destruction, which was breathtaking (Judges 16). The events of this phase of Samson's life are difficult to read, like reading a novel where it quickly becomes obvious that things can't end well for the main character, or like watching a slow-motion train wreck with someone we love onboard. But we humans have a morbid curiosity regarding such events (which television drama producers

The Inextinguishable Blaze

shamelessly exploit). We know we probably shouldn't watch, but we do anyway.

Samson's final journey into personal destruction began with a penchant for prostitutes. The fact that we are not stunned by such a profound moral failure by a leader whose public persona (the uncut hair of a Nazirite) was a lifelong call

> *"Apart from God's chastening and discipline, each of us will eventually destroy with our character what we build with our gift."*

to holiness and separation to God gives silent testimony to our own "jadedness." It's a train wreck, but we're accustomed to train wrecks. They're entertaining to watch, especially if we *"have no skin in the game."* If you and I had been present in Gaza to watch this train wreck we would have seen a Nazirite - a man called to holiness and separation to the God of Israel - visiting a prostitute. When his indiscretion is discovered by his Philistine pursuers he escapes by exercising - even flaunting - his God-given gift. The strength God gave him to save Israel from the Philistines Samson now uses to deliver himself from a visit to a prostitute. Samson picks up the gates of the city (gates, posts and bars) and carries them on His shoulders 40 miles to the town of Hebron. Why? Because he could.

Samson's eventual (even inevitable) downfall came at the hands of another prostitute, named Delilah. Unaddressed character flaws have a cumulative effect on people's lives. Apart from God's chastening and discipline, each of us will eventually destroy with our character what we build with our gift. It is true of you, it is true of me, and it was true of Samson. Samson's moral weakness, his lack of personal discipline, his lack of respect for his own calling, his flaunting of his gift and his contempt for his enemies eventually created the perfect storm of opportunity for the Philistines. When Samson finally confided the source of his strength to Delilah and allowed himself to be shorn, his lack of holiness caught up with him. In the blindness of his deeply flawed character, Samson expected to once again flaunt his gift and escape disaster as he had always done. But it was not to be. Instead, the writer of Judges pens the most dreaded words that any of us can hear spoken about us, *"But he did not know that the LORD had left him"* (Judges 16:20). Samson was captured by the Philistines who gouged out his eyes and shackled him to a grist mill to grind grain like a dumb animal. His descent from holiness to slavery was now complete.

But hair grows back. How long that process took we do not know. Perhaps about as long as it took for a humbled Samson to understand that his strength came, not from his hair, but from God, *"Then Samson called to the LORD and said, 'O Lord GOD, please remember me and please strengthen me only this once, O God, that I may be avenged on the Philistines for my two eyes.'"* (Judges 16:28) It wasn't a particularly eloquent prayer, nor was it spiritually "deep." It was the prayer of a defeated, blinded and humiliated man who was rediscovering that the Nazirite work of true holiness and separation must be lived out *"not by might, nor by power, but by My Spirit says the Lord of Hosts"* (Zechariah 4:6).

"And Samson said, 'Let me die with the Philistines.' Then he bowed with all his strength, and the house fell upon the lords and upon all the people who were in it. So the dead whom he killed at his death were more than those whom he had killed during his life." (Judges 16:30)

Lessons In Holiness For A Samson-like Church

The life of Samson offers us some valuable lessons concerning holiness, devotion, gifting and character if we will

The Inextinguishable Blaze

take the time to listen. And it is vitally important that we take the time, because we have a Church today which increasingly looks more like Samson than Samuel . . . or Jesus.[50]

In the world of politics and politicians we are told with increasing frequency that personal character is only incidental to one's qualifications for public service. We are told that "Does he have a vision" is a more relevant question than "Does he have a mistress." We are assured that personal morals and failings shouldn't necessarily stand in the way of a man's rise to greatness.

Unfortunately, this attitude is quickly pervading the Church, with the result that we are seeing more Samsons than Samuels on display (and Jesus seems nowhere to be found). Mega-Church pastors accused of homosexual relationships with young men under their care remain in their positions and assure their congregations that all is well because they were able to reach an out-of-court financial settlement that will be covered by the Church's insurance. Tattooed healing evangelists who punch, kick and slap demons out of victims are elevated to prominence by Christian media and receive public endorsements by Christian leaders who do so with knowledge of adulterous affairs and alcoholism. Teams of Christian body builders and martial arts practitioners break baseball bats across their knees, break handcuffs behind their backs and plow headlong through walls of burning 2X4s

---

[50]Jesus needs no explanation. Samuel is one of the three Nazirites from birth described in Scripture (Samson and John the Baptist being the other two). He was everything that Samson was not. He was a prophet, not a judge. His life was characterized by genuine holiness and devotion to God, so much so that the people of Israel took note of it: *"And all Israel from Dan to Beersheba knew that Samuel was established as a prophet of the LORD."* (1 Samuel 3:20).

Samson: Holiness, Character And Gifting

as "evangelistic stunts" while their private lives unravel into divorce and bankruptcy, making headlines for internet bloggers who ridicule both them and Christianity. I could cite numerous other prominent examples (and so could you), but these are sufficient to make our point. Samson is alive and well in the Church today, and the consuming fire of God's presence and holiness seems nowhere to be found.

Samson and his modern-day counterparts provide living examples of what happens when the Church allows alleged "spiritual power" or "anointing" or "supernatural calling" or "profound gifting" to trump God's call to character and

> *"Samson is the biblical arch-type of a called and gifted person who destroys with his character what he builds with his gift."*

holiness. Samson is the biblical arch-type of a called and gifted person who destroys with his character what he builds with his gift. Neither calling nor gifting nor anointing can deliver us from the unredeemed flaws of our character any more than they delivered Samson from his. Samson was called and gifted as a Nazirite, but the weaknesses of his character got in the way and eventually proved his undoing.

The excuses most frequently offered to justify such bad behavior and astounding lack of God's holiness include such things as *"He has such a powerful call upon his life"* (so did Samson), or *"He walks in such a powerful anointing"* (so did Samson), or *"He is accomplishing such amazing things"* (so did Samson) or *"He's God's chosen man"* (so was Samson). In fact, almost every excuse that is offered today to justify the modern day "Samsons" of the church could have been offered to defend the Samson who frequented a prostitute in Gaza. What is often overlooked both then and now is that Samson ended his career in disgrace. The best epitaph that

The Inextinguishable Blaze

the writer of Scripture could muster in his defense was that *"the dead whom he killed at his death were more than those whom he had killed during his life."* In other words, Samson's great achievement was that He killed just over 4,000

> *"The lesson of Samson reminds us that the chastisements of God for our violations of His call to holiness can be severe."*

Philistines. Did he "save" Israel for God? Hardly. The remaining five chapters of the Book of Judges record the rapid spiral of Israel into spiritual adultery, idolatry, and social chaos. Spiritually speaking, killing more Philistines represented the least of their problems.

The lesson of Samson reminds us that the chastisements of God for our violations of His call to holiness can be severe. The gifts, the power and the anointings of God belong to Him. They are merely on loan to us so that He can use us to accomplish His greater purposes. They cannot excuse bad behavior and a lack of holiness on our part. When we forget Who God is and who we are in relation to him; when we violate the calling He has placed upon us and forget the purpose for which He called us; when we fail to treat Him as holy in the eyes of others, the consuming fire of God's presence and holiness must respond for His own glory sake.

The Inextinguishable Blaze

It is time to reject the "Samsons" of the Church, along with the pseudo-arguments offered in their defense. We do not need "Samsons" who can wow the crowds by breaking stacks of bricks with their heads. We need "Samuels" who know the voice of God and who daily walk in the consuming fire of His Presence and holiness. It is time for the Church to once again embrace holiness and character as the

Samson: Holiness, Character And Gifting

foundation for profound gifting and anointing. It is time to embrace *"the Inextinguishable Blaze"* of the God Whose presence and holiness are "a consuming fire" in the midst of His people. A failure of holiness proved to be Samson's undoing, and it will prove to be the undoing of the Church in our generation if we fail to embrace"the Inextinguishable Blaze."

"O give me Samuel's ear,
The open ear, O Lord,
Alive and quick to hear
Each whisper of Thy Word,
Like him to answer at Thy call,
And to obey Thee first of all." [51]

The world of our generation is perishing because it has yet to see the fire and the power of a genuinely holy and obedient Church. Are you prepared to show it to them, or are you content to be a "Samson," rather than a "Samuel"?

---

[51] *"Hushed Was The Evening Hymn,"* by James D. Burns.

The Inextinguishable Blaze

Chapter 10

Uzziah: Lessons In Pride And Holiness

Earlier in this book we discussed the importance of thinking right thoughts about God and why, as Tozer observed, *"What comes into our minds when we think about God is the most important thing about us."*[52] Simply put, our view of God impacts our worship, our view of ourselves and our ministries, and how we live out our lives in the world around us. And, yes, it even impacts the behavior of Kings, like King Uzziah of Judah. His wrong thoughts about God eventually got him into trouble with the fire of God's holiness, and that's a story we need to consider.

How Wrong Thoughts About God Got Uzziah Into Trouble

We find the story of King Uzziah's life in the Old Testament book of 2 Chronicles (Chapter 26). The writer of Chronicles likes to divide the Kings of Israel (the Northern Kingdom) and Judah (the Southern Kingdom) into two groups: good kings and bad kings. A good king is one who *"did right in the sight of the Lord,"* whereas a bad king is one who *"did evil in the sight of the LORD."* Uzziah was regarded as a good king, but as we will see, he was a King with "issues." His father, Amaziah, who became King at the age of twenty five, was regarded as a good king who *"did right in the sight of the LORD, yet not with a whole heart."* Amaziah's reign and life had ended poorly, and his young son, Uzziah came to the throne at the age of sixteen.

What follows here is not a detailed exposition of Uzziah's life.

---

[52] A. W. Tozer, *The Knowledge of the Holy* (Harper & Row: New York, 1961), page 9

The Inextinguishable Blaze

Rather, the following represents my observations in light of our topic of holiness, the fear of God and thinking right thoughts about God.

"Uzziah was sixteen years old when he became king, and he reigned fifty-two years in Jerusalem; and his mother's name was Jechiliah of Jerusalem. And he did right in the sight of the Lord according to all that his father Amaziah had done. And he continued to seek God in the days of Zechariah, who had understanding through the vision of God; and as long as he sought the Lord, God prospered him." (26:3-5)

God prospered Uzziah as long as Uzziah sought Him. God prospered Uzziah, although we are never told exactly what that prosperity consisted of. And that's the challenge. We don't get to define what "prosperity" means. God does. The modern proponents of "the prosperity gospel" have usurped the conversation by defining prosperity in terms of material and financial prosperity. And while the Kingdom of Judah under Uzziah's reign certainly prospered materially and financially, success and prosperity are always on God's terms, not ours.

We must not miss the fact that the roots of Uzziah's eventual downfall found fertile ground in Uzziah's outward success. We assume that outward success is a sign of God's blessing. Yet, I have met very few people who

"Success is a wonderful blessing, but it is a poor teacher."

learned important spiritual lessons from their success. When people are successful they usually don't' ask God *"Why did this happen to me?"* (A point made over a generation ago by G.K. Chesterton in "Orthodoxy"). Most important life lessons are learned from our failures, because failure has a tendency to drive us to our knees in search of both answers and

Uzziah: Lessons In Pride And Holiness

mercy. Don't misunderstand me at this point. Success is a wonderful blessing, but it is a poor teacher. And one of the ways we begin thinking wrong thoughts about God is by misinterpreting our own success.

There is haunting foreboding in the statement, *"as long as he sought the Lord, God prospered him."* The day would soon come when Uzziah's faith would falter and expose a character weakness that no one had expected.

"Moreover, Uzziah prepared for all the army shields, spears, helmets, body armor, bows and sling stones. And in Jerusalem he made engines of war invented by skillful men to be on the towers and on the corners, for the purpose of shooting arrows and great stones. Hence his fame spread afar, for he was marvelously helped until he was strong." (26:14-15)

God helped Uzziah until his strength got in the way. If you're feeling weak right now, there's good news: God loves to help the weak. But if you're feeling strong, I've got some bad news. God may not be in it. One of the ways we begin thinking wrong thoughts about God is by listening to and believing our own publicity. Our "fame" goes to our head and we begin thinking less about God's greatness and more about our own blessing. We still do lip service to God as the source of our blessing, but it is a hollow refrain. The awful reality is we have come to think too much of ourselves and our gifts while thinking too little about God and His holiness.

"But when he became strong, his heart was so proud that he acted corruptly, and he was unfaithful to the Lord his God, for he entered the temple of the Lord to burn incense on the altar of incense" (26:16)

The Inextinguishable Blaze

Pride will turn your greatest blessing into your greatest curse. By now it was obvious that Uzziah was both strong and blessed. And that was the beginning of wrong thinking about God. Strength and blessing can do strange things to people. Together they become fertilizer for the weeds of pride.

Pride caused Uzziah to think wrong thoughts about God and to violate His holiness. Uzziah's worst wrong thought about God was that God's laws of "holiness-by-separation" didn't apply to him.

> *"Uzziah confused God's blessing with God's approval."*

Uzziah had been so successful as King, his pride told him there was no reason why he couldn't be a great priest, too! While the Old Testament laws of "holiness-by-separation" prohibited such a thing, Uzziah's pride told him that he was above those laws. Uzziah's pride led him to a second wrongful thought about God and to a mistake that is common among gifted people: Uzziah confused God's blessing with God's approval.

Both then and now - Old Testament and New - God calls fallen sinful men to serve Him. In the process He gives them spiritual gifts along with the anointing of power necessary to exercise them effectively. He may even grant them outward success and prosperity. But one of the ways we begin thinking wrong thoughts about God is by confusing His gifts, anointings and blessings in our lives with His approval of all our beliefs, our opinions and our lifestyles. Don't confuse God's blessing with God's approval of your character flaws. Uzziah did, and it cost him dearly.

"Then Azariah the priest entered after him and with him eighty priests of the Lord, valiant men. And they opposed Uzziah the king and said to him, 'It is not for you, Uzziah, to

Uzziah: Lessons In Pride And Holiness

burn incense to the Lord, but for the priests, the sons of Aaron who are consecrated to burn incense. Get out of the sanctuary, for you have been unfaithful, and will have no honor from the Lord God.' But Uzziah, with a censer in his hand for burning incense, was enraged; and while he was enraged with the priests, the leprosy broke out on his forehead before the priests in the house of the Lord, beside the altar of incense." (26:17-19)

Pride causes us to forget who God is, who we are in relation to Him, and what He has called us to do. Uzziah was called to be King; He wasn't called to be a priest. Strength and blessing combined with pride to create wrong thoughts about God. Strength and blessing combined with pride to cause Uzziah to forget who he was, who God was, and what he had been called to do.

> *"When we forget God's place, we quickly become confused about our own place."*

Wrong thoughts about God will result in a wrong understanding of who we are in relation to Him. When we forget God's place, we quickly become confused about our own place.

Uzziah's actions represented a serious breach of God's holiness. Not only had he violated the Priestly office and function, but by doing so he had failed to treat God as holy and to honor Him as holy before others. As with Nadab and Abihu, and Moses and Aaron, God responded quickly and severely to this breach of His holiness. Uzziah was struck with leprosy on his forehead, the very place where Priests were required to wear a gold plate inscribed with "Holy to the Lord." (See Exodus 28:36-38).

"And Azariah the chief priest and all the priests looked at

The Inextinguishable Blaze

him, and behold, he was leprous on his forehead; and they hurried him out of there, and he himself also hastened to get out because the Lord had smitten him. And King Uzziah was a leper to the day of his death; and he lived in a separate house, being a leper, for he was cut off from the house of the Lord. And Jotham his son was over the king's house judging the people of the land." (26:20-21)

Uzziah received a costly lesson regarding holiness and the fear of the Lord. The text tells us that Uzziah *"hastened to get out because the Lord had smitten him."* My impression is that Uzziah was smitten not only with leprosy, but with fear - the fear of God which results from a personal confrontation with the God Who is holy. The fear of God reminds us of two things. It reminds us of who God is - a holy God who is not to be trifled with. It also reminds us of who we are in relation to Him - servants called to holiness and obedience. The fear of God breaks our pride and places us in right relationship to God and His holiness, and to the world around us. The fear of God restores God to His proper place, restores us to our proper place and causes us to once again think rightly about ourselves, about God, and about His purposes in the world. All of this happened to King Uzziah in a moment's time. And it cost him dearly, *"And King Uzziah was a leper to the day of his death; and he lived in a separate house, being a leper, for he was cut off from the house of the Lord."*

The Inextinguishable Blaze

It is time for the Church of our generation to once again embrace the truth that the most important thing about any man or woman is what he or she thinks about God, not what he or she thinks about themselves (Pride). It was true of Uzziah, and it is true of us as well. When Uzziah failed to think of God as holy, he forgot who he was in relation to God. As a result he also failed to treat God as holy in the eyes of

Uzziah: Lessons In Pride And Holiness

others. All of this combined to produce disastrous consequences for himself and for Israel. The same is true today. When the Church fails to pursue and embrace *"the Inextinguishable Blaze"* of God's presence and holiness, we forget who we are in relation to God. As a result we also fail to treat Him as holy in the eyes of a watching world, with disastrous consequences. The life and lessons of Uzziah would provide the backdrop for one of God's greatest revelations of Himself and His holiness in all of Scripture. That revelation would take place *"In the year of King Uzziah's death."* Sometimes God uses the experience of others to open our eyes so that we can see.

And that is the story we need to tell next.

The Inextinguishable Blaze

Chapter 11

Isaiah And the God Who Is "Holy, Holy, Holy"

*"Holy, Holy, Holy, is the Lord of hosts,
The whole earth is full of His glory."*

Certain truths bear repeating, and this is one of them: The most important thing about any man or woman is what he or she thinks about God. This spiritual truth has shaped the lives of God's people for thousands of years. In the previous chapter we saw this truth worked out in the life of King Uzziah. Now we will see its impact upon the life of the Prophet Isaiah.

A quick look at Isaiah 6:1-8 reveals four truths each of us must know to truly walk, serve and minister in the Kingdom of God: 1) We need to know God for Who He is, not for who we imagine Him to be; 2) We need to know who we are in relation to this God; 3) We need to know what He has done for us; 4) We need to know what He is calling us to do. These four issues are at the heart of the Church in every generation, including ours. These four truths and our response to them will determine the DNA of the Church for the next generation. This means they are of more than mere passing interest. I do not claim any unique insights on this passage. Rather, I come to this passage as one working to come to terms with its meaning and significance in my own life. What follows here are my personal reflections.

Here's Who God Is - He is "Holy" (Isaiah 6:1-4)

In the year of King Uzziah's death, I saw the Lord sitting on a throne, lofty and exalted, with the train of His robe filling the temple. Seraphim stood above Him, each having six wings; with two he covered his face, and with two he covered his feet, and with two he flew. And one called out to another and

The Inextinguishable Blaze

said, 'Holy, Holy, Holy, is the Lord of hosts, The whole earth is full of His glory.' And the foundations of the thresholds trembled at the voice of him who called out, while the temple was filling with smoke.

King Uzziah, whose life we examined in our previous chapter, died in the year 740 B.C., having reigned for 52 years and having presided over decades of national prosperity. Isaiah had already been a prophet for several years prior to King Uzziah's death. While we can never know the full extent to which the life and lessons of King Uzziah affected the young prophet, we can be certain that they did. Why? Because it was Isaiah himself who cited Uzziah's death as the mile marker in his own life for what happened next.

Whether or not Isaiah was actually in the Temple in Jerusalem when he experienced this vision we do not know. All we know is what he saw: a vision of Jehovah - Isaiah's God - seated as King upon a throne in His temple, *"lofty and exalted"* (i.e., *"transcendent"*). His royal robe filled the temple with its train. And in His regal transcendence Jehovah was attended by six-winged angels known as "seraphim" whose worship refrain rang out and filled the temple: *"Holy, Holy, Holy, is the Lord of hosts, The whole earth is full of His glory."*

Isaiah's description of His vision is a near copy of what occurred on Mt. Sinai when the God of holiness visited Israel there. Substitute trembling *"foundations of the thresholds"* for a mountain shaking at the voice of God, substitute a temple filling with smoke for fire and smoke upon the mountain and the descriptions are amazingly similar. Some things don't change. Like Moses and the people of God at the foot of Mt. Sinai, Isaiah found himself standing in the presence of the God of Israel Whose Presence and holiness are "a consuming fire," the transcendent God whose glory fills the

Isaiah And The God Who Is Holy Holy Holy

whole earth but transcends it, and Whose holiness is both beautiful and terrifying to look upon.

As we noted earlier in our discussion of the word "holy" (Chapter 5) , Scripture may refer to some things as "holy," and it may describe a few things as "most holy," but only God is *"holy, holy, holy."* No other attribute or characteristic of God's nature is ever referred to this way. While Scripture tells us that "God is love," no where are we ever told that God is "love, love, love." God and holiness are synonymous and inseparable in a way that defies description except for the seraphim to cry, *"Holy, Holy, Holy."*

I would dare say that the vast majority of churches in the western world are led by teachers (as opposed to "pastors"), reflecting our overall "rationalistic" approach to faith. Teachers are one of the 5-fold gifts of Ephesians 4, which means they are important to the overall equipping and

> *"God and holiness are synonymous and inseparable in a way that defies description except for the seraphim to cry, 'Holy, Holy, Holy.'"*

building up of the church. But the weakness of every 5-fold gift lies in the shadow of its strength. The weaknesses of a teacher is that they have never met a problem that couldn't be solved with more teaching. Unfortunately, this approach doesn't work. How do I know? After 35 years of teaching on biblical finances in the church, Christian giving as a percentage has fallen by 35% (yep, 1% each year). There is more teaching on biblical marriage today than at any time in the life of the church, yet our divorce rate is equal to that of the non-church world. Why? Because good teaching alone is inadequate to solve deeply rooted spiritual problems.

The Inextinguishable Blaze

The same could be said of the issue of holiness. You cannot teach your way into the holiness of God any more than you can teach your way into a loving marriage. Like marriage, holiness is relational, not educational. What the Church needs today is not a study on holiness (although there is nothing wrong with good teaching on the subject). What we need is a genuine encounter with the living God before Whom even the angels cover their eyes and declare *"Holy, Holy, Holy, is the Lord of hosts, The whole earth is full of His glory."* That is what Isaiah needed. Although already a Prophet, he needed a fresh vision of God. He needed to see God for Who He is, not for who Isaiah imagined Him to be.[53] And that is what we need, too. Every profound gift needs a profound encounter with God to clarify the calling, to develop the character and to put life and ministry into proper perspective. In the absence of such an encounter men create pseudo-holiness by means of legalistic rules. When holiness becomes a set of *"Rules for Spiritual Behavior"* it isn't long before the rules become veils. Religious legalism is like the veil over Moses' face when the glory of God's presence began to fade. It is man's attempt to convince himself and others that the glory of God's Presence has not departed; that the fire of God's holiness remains, when in reality the fire has gone out and the altar has gone cold.

Here's Who I Am - A Ruined Sinner Saved By Grace (Isaiah 6:5)

"Then I said, 'Woe is me, for I am ruined! Because I am a

---

[53] Just how profound an impact this encounter had upon Isaiah can be found by how he addresses God. Throughout his prophetic ministry Isaiah consistently refers to Jehovah as "the Holy One of Israel." Of the 36 times this phrase appears in the Old Testament, 25 are in the book of Isaiah. For Isaiah, God would always be "the Holy One of Israel."

Isaiah And The God Who Is Holy Holy Holy

man of unclean lips, And I live among a people of unclean lips; For my eyes have seen the King, the Lord of hosts.'"

Earlier (Chapter 8) we noted the two different responses to God's revelation of Himself and His holiness at Mt. Sinai. When the people of Israel were confronted with the demands of God's holiness their response was to shrink back. But Moses, when confronted with the same demands of God's holiness, cried out for more, *"show me Thy glory!"* And each received what they asked for.

But here in Isaiah 6:5 we see a third response. When confronted with the glorious and transcendent holiness of his God and King, Isaiah responded with fear, conviction of sin, self-realization, self-loathing and genuine repentance. In a moment of profound self-awareness Isaiah saw himself in the searing light of God's holiness. In that instant Isaiah saw and understood the difference between God's holiness on the one hand, and his own sin and that of his fellow Israelites on the other hand. In that moment he found himself "undone,"[54] standing naked in the searing light of God's holiness without so much as a fig leaf to hide the reality of his own sin. At such a moment, *"Woe is me!"* is the only possible response of the human heart. In its essence, genuine repentance is the response of

> *". . . genuine repentance is the response of the human heart to an encounter with the God Whose presence and holiness are 'a consuming fire.'"*

---

[54]The Hebrew word rendered "undone" (*damah*) carries the sense of *"to be cut off or cut down, to be brought to silence or to be utterly undone."* The Greek Septuagint rendering of this passage uses the word *katanusso* which communicates the idea of *"to pierce thoroughly, to agitate violently or to sting to the quick."*

The Inextinguishable Blaze

the human heart to an encounter with the God Whose presence and holiness are "a consuming fire."

I am bothered by a trend I see in the church among believers today. It is a trend of self-exaltation. As we observed earlier in Chapter 2, contemporary Western Christianity, particularly in America, has witnessed a slow but massive swing of the theological pendulum, away from a faith and a theology which are "theo-centric" (God-Centered) and toward a faith and theology which are "anthropo-centric" (man-centered). Simply put, we now live in a Church where men have "increased" and God has "decreased" (the exact opposite of John the Baptist's observation in John 3:20). The moral catastrophe of man's fall into sin has been replaced by a contemporary trend of self-exaltation. Such a trend of self-exaltation points to a generation of nominal believers who are infatuated with their own pseudo-significance and who know little or nothing about either the transcendent, exalted and holy God Who confronted the Prophet Isaiah, or the consuming fire of His Presence and holiness. And it goes without saying that they have also lost any sense of the fear of God.

Standing in the undimmed brilliance of God's holiness, Isaiah found himself delivered from any "pseudo-significance" or "self-exaltation." In that moment of divine revelation Isaiah was brought to a fresh and new understanding both of Who God is and of his own status before this exalted and holy God. In that moment, Isaiah understood that he was a sinner dwelling in a nation of sinners. This presented Isaiah with a problem that only God could solve. He needed deliverance from His own unworthiness.

Here's What He Has Done For Me (Isaiah 6:6-7)

"Then one of the seraphim flew to me, with a burning coal in

Isaiah And The God Who Is Holy Holy Holy

his hand which he had taken from the altar with tongs. And he touched my mouth with it and said, 'Behold, this has touched your lips; and your iniquity is taken away, and your sin is forgiven.'"

According to his biographer, James Boswell (*"The Life of Samuel Johnson,"* 1791), Dr. Samuel Johnson once remarked, *"Depend upon it, sir, when a man knows he is to be hanged in a fortnight, it concentrates his mind wonderfully."* Confronting the possibility of one's imminent death - especially at the hands of God Himself as we stand in the fire of His Presence - can wonderfully focus the mind and give us amazing clarity. Just ask Isaiah.

Isaiah discovered what Dr. Johnson could only imagine. He discovered that standing in the Presence of the Holy One of Israel has an amazing effect upon us. It *"clears the sinuses,"* wonderfully concentrates the mind and places everything in its proper perspective. This includes the reality that our own sin and lack of holiness is so great that it requires a divine remedy; a supernatural act on God's part to deal with it and to rescue fallen mankind. The very One Whose holiness

"The God Whose presence and holiness are 'a consuming fire' is also the God and Savior Who redeems us."

demands our judgment and condemnation is the only One Who can provide the remedy for our predicament. Scripture describes this divine solution with imagery and metaphor: fire, burning coals, washings, *"as far as the east is from the west,"*(Psalm 103:12), etc. But they all point to one thing: The God Whose holiness cries out for our condemnation has made it possible for our iniquity to be "taken away" and for our sins to be forgiven. And all of this imagery points to one

The Inextinguishable Blaze

thing: What God Himself has accomplished on our behalf through the atoning death of His Son, Jesus. The God Whose presence and holiness are "a consuming fire" is also the God and Savior Who redeems us.

Here's What He's Calling Me To Do (Isaiah 6:8)

"Then I heard the voice of the Lord, saying, 'Whom shall I send, and who will go for Us?' Then I said, 'Here am I. Send me!'"

Evangelical believers have an unfortunate tendency which I have noticed over the years. We want to skip to the conclusion before understanding the argument. John Wesley put it another way when he observed that the reason we are not more holy is because we are "enthusiasts" who seek the "ends" without the "means." A. W. Tozer made a similar observation in his book, *"The Root of the Righteous."* We want results without roots. We then bemoan the reality that our results, our "fruit," don't last. Why don't they last? Because they had no roots.

With respect to Isaiah Chapter 6, the Church wants the result found here in verse 8 without having to work through verses 1-7. Having been a believer and a participant in the organized church for some 44 years now, I have heard innumerable "missions" messages built around this verse, all of which close with an exhortation that we need to tell God to "send me." But to use this verse out of context is to rob the passage of its spiritual power. It wasn't until Isaiah saw God for Who He truly is in all of His "terrible holiness," understood who he was in relation to this God and what this God of Holiness had done for him, that Isaiah was in a mental and spiritual position to answer the call and to say "send me." It was a personal encounter with the Holy One of Israel Whose Presence and holiness are *"a consuming fire,"* an encounter

Isaiah And The God Who Is Holy Holy Holy

which produced a genuine "fear of the Lord," that motivated Isaiah to "go." And before we conclude that people being motivated by "the fear of the Lord" is another one of those Old testament "quirks," we might want to talk to the Apostle Paul. Writing to believers in the Greek city of Corinth the Apostle Paul revealed the motivation behind His own Apostolic ministry: *"Therefore, knowing the fear of the Lord, we persuade men . . . ."* (2 Corinthians 5:11). Does the "love of Christ" control, constrain and motivate us? Yes, it does, just as Paul states four verses later in 2 Corinthians 5:14. But so does God's holiness and fear. As Isaiah (and Paul) discovered, holiness and the fear of the Lord motivate people to a life of obedience and service in a way that no amount of teaching or cajoling ever could. No amount of teaching can produce this kind of obedience. It cannot be taught. Like fire, it must be caught.

The Inextinguishable Blaze

It is time for the Church of our generation to rediscover the God of Isaiah and the Scriptures Who is *"holy, holy holy"* and before Whom even the angels bow in worship with covered faces. For me, this is personal. Several years ago, my wife and I were treated by friends to a 10-day vacation. One morning during our stay the Holy Spirit woke me up at around 4:45 AM to pray. As I sat in the early morning quiet of the condo, praying and watching the sunrise, the Lord spoke very clearly: *"I am going to give My Church an Isaiah 6 experience of my holiness."* The word was as clear as any I have ever received. It is consistent with Scripture, with other similar words I have received and with the recorded experience of God's Church during times of historic spiritual awakening. It is time for the Church to pursue *"the inextinguishable blaze,"* and to do so in the assurance that He has promised to meet us along the way.

The Inextinguishable Blaze

Chapter 12

Holiness And The Church of God

*"But a certain man named Ananias, with his wife Sapphira, sold a piece of property, and kept back some of the price for himself, with his wife's full knowledge, and bringing a portion of it, he laid it at the apostles' feet. But Peter said, 'Ananias, why has Satan filled your heart to lie to the Holy Spirit, and to keep back some of the price of the land? While it remained unsold, did it not remain your own? And after it was sold, was it not under your control? Why is it that you have conceived this deed in your heart? You have not lied to men, but to God.' And as he heard these words, Ananias fell down and breathed his last; and **great fear** came upon all who heard of it. . . . . And she fell immediately at his feet, and breathed her last; and the young men came in and found her dead, and they carried her out and buried her beside her husband. And **great fear** came upon the whole church, and upon all who heard of these things."* (Acts 5:1-11)

The God of Holiness, Old and New

Throughout the past eleven chapters of this book we have labored carefully to tie the biblical concept of holiness in the Old Testament to the same concept in the New Testament. There is an important reason for this: God hasn't changed. God is as holy in the New Testament as He ever was in the Old.

We need to be clear on this point. Jesus didn't come to save us from the wrath of the holy-but-angry God of the Old Testament. That would be like saying that He came to save us from Himself. Our doctrine of the trinity (three-in-one and one-in-three) forbids such a contradictory and foolish idea. Jesus Himself declared *"I and the Father are one"* (John 10:30, the use of the neuter communicates the sense of "one

The Inextinguishable Blaze

in essence"). To state this truth in simple terms, when it comes to this matter of "holiness" the three Persons of the triune God are all "on the same page." The triune God of the New Testament - Father, Son and Holy Spirit - is just as holy and just as fearful as He has always been. The difference is the cross of Christ.

In the New Testament God is now approachable, but He is still Holy. The difference is the Cross of Christ where the enmity of God's wrath toward sin has been mollified (the biblical word is "propitiated")

"God hasn't changed. God is as holy in the New Testament as He ever was in the Old."

through the sacrificial death of Christ for sin. This involves the subject of "reconciliation" which is part of our evangelical doctrine of the Atonement. Reconciliation refers to that change in God's attitude toward sinful men as a result of Christ's sacrificial death. Theologians refer to this as "Objective Reconciliation." As Henry Thiessen writes, [55]

"The thought is something like this: At first God and man stood face to face with each other. In sinning, Adam turned his back upon God. Then God turned His back upon Adam. Christ's death has satisfied the demands of God and now God has again turned His face toward man. It remains for man to turn round about and face God. Since God has been reconciled by the death of His son, man is now entreated to be reconciled to God. In the largest sense of that word, God has reconciled to Himself not only man, but also all things in heaven and on earth" (Colossians 1:20)

---

[55]Henry Clarence Thiessen, **Introductory Lectures In Systematic Theology** (Grand Rapids: William B. Eerdmans Publishing Company, 1949), page 328.

Holiness And The Church Of God

The wrath of God in the Old Testament represented the personal response of a holy God to the personal affront of sin against His holiness. Remember. Holiness is personal. It always has been . .

"In the New Testament God is now approachable, but He is still Holy."

. and it always will be. God is as holy today as He was upon Mt. Sinai. The difference is the reconciliation brought about as a result of Christ's sacrificial death. The veil of the Temple separating the Holy of Holies from the Holy Place - the violation of which cost Nadab and Abihu their lives at the hands of God's holy wrath - has been torn from top to bottom (Matthew 27:51; Mark 15:38; Luke 23:45) signifying that we now have access to God's very Presence by faith through the atoning sacrifice of Jesus on the cross. God remains holy, but His wrath has been mollified by the reconciliation brought about through the atoning death of Jesus. Mollified? Yes. Eliminated? Not quite. Just ask Ananias and Sapphira.

The Lesson Of Ananias And Sapphira

The lesson of Ananias and Sapphira (found in Acts 5:1-11) reminds us that God remains "a consuming fire" of holiness in the midst of His people. It also teaches us to take His holiness seriously. To forget this truth is to think wrong thoughts about God, with disastrous consequences. Just ask Ananias and Sapphira.

The circumstances surrounding this incident involved believers (like Barnabas) donating property to meet the growing needs of the early Church (Acts 4:36-37). At that time a husband and wife in the Jerusalem Church named Ananias and Sapphira also sold a piece of property and made a donation to the Church. But they chose to keep a portion of the proceeds from the sale for themselves while

The Inextinguishable Blaze

publicly claiming to have donated the entire amount to the Church. Simply put, they lied and deceived. When Peter (operating under prophetic insight) confronted them in the presence of witnesses they publicly lied both to men and - more importantly - to God (Acts 5:4).

In response to this personal affront to His holiness, God struck both Ananias and Sapphira dead on the spot (first Ananias, then Sapphira four hours later). If God's response in this situation looks and sounds vaguely familiar, it should. We have

> *"Reconciliation has mollified the wrath of God toward men in general, but He is as holy as He has ever been."*

seen it before. We saw it in the case of Nadab and Abihu. It is the response of God in the consuming fire of His holiness toward those who fail to treat and honor Him as holy before others. In a way that no amount of teaching could ever do, the incident of Ananias and Sapphira links the consuming fire of God's holiness in the Old Testament to His holiness in the New Testament. Reconciliation has mollified the wrath of God toward men in general, but He is as holy as He has ever been. His wrath remains as His personal response to those who willfully violate His holiness and who fail to honor and treat Him as holy in the eyes of others.

By their behavior in this matter Ananias and Sapphira failed to treat and honor God as holy in the eyes of others. By His response to their actions God solved that problem, as we read in verse 11, *"And **great fear** came upon the whole church, and upon all who heard of these things."* God's response to this willful violation of His holiness had a two-pronged impact. The first impact was that "great fear" fell upon "the whole church." As we observed earlier in this book, the biblical reality is that fear teaches us things that we cannot (or will not) learn any other way. Fear shatters our comfort zones and causes our hearts to tremble, *"so that all the people who were in the camp trembled."* (Exodus 19:16) The trembling heart is a teachable heart. As a result of this incident with Ananias and Sapphira the Jerusalem Church of the Book of Acts gained a teachable heart and received a valuable lesson which they would not soon forget. It was Mt. Sinai, Nadab and Abihu, and Isaiah in the Temple all rolled into one. But there was more.

The second impact of God's response to this violation of His holiness was that "*great fear*" fell upon *"all who heard of these things."* In other words, people outside the Church (i.e., unbelievers) heard about what God had done within the Church to Ananias and Sapphira. Suddenly, for believer and unbeliever alike, the Church had become a supernatural and powerful - even dangerous - community which worshiped a God Whose Presence and holiness were "a consuming fire." He was not to be trifled with. Lie to Him in the presence of others and you might just drop dead on the spot. It had happened (twice, actually), and it could happen again.

Holiness, Gifts and Signs and Wonders

"And at the hands of the apostles many signs and wonders were taking place among the people; and they were all with one accord in Solomon's portico. But none of the rest dared to associate with them; however, the people held them in high esteem." (Acts 5:12-13)

The early church may have been hated by some (i.e., the Jewish religious leaders), and even feared by others as a potential threat (i.e., the Roman political establishment), but following the episode of Ananias and Sapphira something else happened to the reputation of the Church: *"the people held them in high esteem."* A literal rendering of the Greek

The Inextinguishable Blaze

text in verse 13 might read like this, *"the rest (of the people) did not have the courage to join them, but the people made a big deal about them."* The episode of Ananias and Sapphira struck such fear into "the people" (i.e., unbelievers) that many of them simply did not have the "courage" to join themselves to the Christian community. After all, what if they joined the Christian community and God struck them dead? But at the same time "the people" made such a big deal about what had happened in the Church that this episode became "the talk of the town." But there was more.

"And all the more believers in the Lord, multitudes of men and women, were constantly added to their number; to such an extent that they even carried the sick out into the streets, and laid them on cots and pallets, so that when Peter came by, at least his shadow might fall on any one of them. And also the people from the cities in the vicinity of Jerusalem were coming together, bringing people who were sick or afflicted with unclean spirits; and they were all being healed." (Acts 5:14-16)

God's actions in the matter of Ananias and Sapphira had a third impact which we see here in verse 14, namely, powerful evangelism - *"multitudes of men and women, were constantly added to their number."* Yes, some people were so struck with fear that they avoided associating with the Christians (at least initially), but it appears that many more ("multitudes") were brought to faith.

At this point we need to reflect on the order of events in this chapter. Acts Chapter 5 divides into two parts. Part one (5:1-11) records the episode of Ananias and Sapphira. Part 2 (5:12-16) records the impact of that episode upon "the people" (i.e., unbelievers). Part 1 emphasizes the holiness of God, while Part 2 emphasizes the "power" of God as manifested through signs and wonders. I believe that there

Holiness And The Church Of God

is a reason for this order of events, and this deserves our attention.

Someone once observed that you and I will destroy with our character what we build with our gift. We saw this played out in the life of Samson (Chapter 9). Holiness is about character, not

"Holiness is about character, not gifting."

gifting. Holiness is about us embracing the consuming fire of God's Presence and allowing that fire to align our character with His. As we observed earlier in this book, genuine holiness is about Who you worship, Who you love and Whose image is transforming your life. Holiness begins with God and ends with us being transformed into His image.

The consuming fire of God's holiness, as experienced by the Church and as witnessed by "the people," set the stage both for greater evangelism and for the accompanying demonstrations of God's power through signs and wonders. Signs and

"Signs and wonders without holiness represent gifts without character. They will eventually destroy both the person and the Church."

wonders without holiness represent gifts without character. They will eventually destroy both the person and the Church. This passage suggests to all who will listen that there is an order to what God seeks to do. When we violate that order we fail to treat God as holy and we threaten our own destruction.

Signs and wonders may "wow" the crowd for a brief season (just as they did for the Children of Israel in the Book of Exodus), but the consuming fire of God's Presence and

The Inextinguishable Blaze

holiness will instill "great fear" in the hearts of believers and unbelievers alike and will cause unbelievers to once again "make a big deal" about what God is doing in His Church. And that will set the stage for "*multitudes of men and women*" coming to faith and experiencing God's power in signs and wonders. To confuse this order is to confuse character and gifting, and people so confused will eventually destroy themselves . . . and the Church. Perhaps this is what Jesus meant when he warned His disciples,

"Not everyone who says to me, 'Lord, Lord,' will enter the kingdom of heaven, but the one who does the will of my Father who is in heaven. On that day many will say to me, 'Lord, Lord, did we not prophesy in your name, and cast out demons in your name, and do many mighty works in your name?' And then will I declare to them, 'I never knew you; depart from me, you workers of lawlessness.'" (Matthew 7:21-23)

Holiness And Love

The culture of the Evangelical Church has emphasized the attribute of God's love to the point of nearly excluding everything else that is true about the nature and person of God. Both the Christian and the unbeliever could easily conclude from this emphasis that "love" is God's ONLY attribute, or at the least they might conclude that love is His most important attribute. Both conclusions would be wrong.

As we observed earlier in Chapter 5, while Scripture tells us that "God is love," no where are we ever told that God is "love, love, love." God and holiness are synonymous and inseparable in a way that defies description except for the seraphim to cry, *"holy, holy, holy."* It would be wrong for us to conclude that "holy" or "holiness" simply describes one of God's many wonderful characteristics or attributes. Rather, this is what philosophers and theologians would characterize as an "existential" statement: one that defines God's very existence, the very nature of His essential being.[56]

"Holy" defines and describes God's essential nature in a way that nothing else does. The practical impact of this is that everything God does is "holy." And that includes His love. If you doubt this truth, just ask Jesus. Through His

"In Jesus, love becomes holiness expressed, and holiness becomes love made pure."

sacrificial death and atonement on the Cross, Jesus paid the high price of holiness so that the love of God could be shed abroad in our hearts by the Holy Spirit. The love and the holiness of God met in the person of Christ, and through His sacrificial atoning death the wrath of God has been mollified so that believers today can carry *"the Inextinguishable Blaze"* of His presence without being destroyed by it.

In Jesus, love becomes holiness expressed, and holiness becomes love made pure.

In his book ***The Cost of Discipleship*** German theologian and martyr Dietrich Bonhoeffer wrote about "cheap grace" which he explained as follows:

"cheap grace is the preaching of forgiveness without requiring repentance, baptism without church discipline. Communion without confession. Cheap grace is grace

---

[56]The phrase "God is love" appears twice in Scripture (1 John 4:8 & 16). The phrase "God is a consuming fire" also occurs twice (Deuteronomy 4:24 and Hebrews 12:29), and the phrase "God is holy" appears once (Psalm 99:9). The point here is that we cannot define God's essential nature by "counting verses."

The Inextinguishable Blaze

without discipleship, grace without the cross, grace without Jesus Christ." [57]

Writing about the Church of the 1930s and 40s Bonhoeffer was right about *"cheap grace."* Today, more than a half-century later the Evangelical Church of the early 21st Century has gone beyond "cheap grace." We now offer "cheap love" - God's love without the consuming fire of God's holiness. When the Church ignores or minimizes God's holiness in favor of His love, the result is to cheapen God's love, to minimize the price holiness paid for that love in the death of Christ and to offend His holiness. And as we have seen throughout this book, offending God's holiness can have disastrous consequences.

Love God And Do What?

"Love God and do whatever you please: for the soul trained in love to God will do nothing to offend the One who is Beloved." St. Augustine of Hippo

In our treatment of holiness in the Old Testament we discovered that the purpose of God's rules and laws as laid out in the 612 requirements of the Law and all of the religious rituals and ordinances of "separation" was two-fold. First, their regular observance served to remind His people of the extent of His holiness. The outward, ritual requirements of God's holiness affected nearly every area of their daily lives. Second, the observance of those laws, rituals and ordinances of "separation" prevented the Israelites from being consumed by the fire of His Presence as they went about their daily lives with the Presence of God in their midst.

---

[57]Dietrich Bonhoeffer, **The Cost of Discipleship** (New York: Macmillan, 1966).

Holiness And The Church Of God

Simply stated, holiness in the Old Testament was primarily about outward "separation." This reality fundamentally changed in the New Testament when love and holiness met and reconciliation was accomplished in the cross of Christ. From that point forward, holiness changed from outward separation to inward transformation (Paul's point in 2 Corinthians 3). Unlike Nadab and Abihu, Ananias and Sapphira were not struck down for violating some physical veil of priestly separation. The Old Testament Laws of Separation no longer defined holiness. They were struck down for a lack of inward transformation as evidenced by willfully lying to the Holy Spirit.

This fundamental shift from outward separation to inward transformation is the truth which underlies the decision of the Apostles and elders in Acts 15. There the Apostolic leadership of the early Church decided against requiring gentile believers to keep the "law of Moses" with all of its outward requirements of separation. The times and seasons had changed. Through His sacrificial death Jesus had perfectly fulfilled all of the outward requirements of the law. From that point onward, the focus would be upon inward transformation and the work of the Holy Spirit to inscribe the law upon the hearts of men. Which brings us to St. Augustine.

When St. Augustine, Bishop of Hippo, penned those now-famous words some sixteen hundred years ago, he expressed the practical side of New Testament holiness. I am convinced that Augustine understood (better than most believers today) that in Jesus, love becomes holiness expressed and holiness becomes love made pure. The professing believer who truly walks in the love of this God Whose presence and holiness are "a consuming fire" will, in the words of Augustine, *"do nothing to offend the One who is Beloved."* And if Ananias and Sapphira had walked in this type of love and holiness, Acts Chapter 5 would never have taken place.

The Inextinguishable Blaze

It is time for the Church to embrace the reality that God is as holy in the New Testament as He ever was in the Old Testament, but it is a holiness that is now manifested and expressed primarily through inward transformation rather than outward separation.

It is time for the Church to reject that "cheap love" which divorces God's love from the fire of His holiness. In Jesus, love and holiness have met and reconciliation has been accomplished. As a result, in Jesus, love becomes holiness expressed and holiness becomes love made pure. And that is good news indeed.

"A person repents when he comes to the place where he discovers that the will of God is the government of his life and the glory of God is the reason for his life. He only has repented who has changed his mind about his reason for being." - Paris Reidhead

"Some people do not like to hear much of repentance; but I think it is so necessary that if I should die in the pulpit, I would desire to die preaching repentance, and if out of the pulpit I would desire to die practicing it." - Matthew Henry

"Repentance, to be of any avail, must work a change of heart and conduct." - Theodore Ledyard Cuyler

"Neither is repentance a one-time act. It is a lifestyle, an ongoing commitment to keep putting aside our rebellion and receive God's forgiveness." - Bruce Wilkinson

"We talk religion in a world that worships the bread but does not distribute it, that practices ritual rather than righteousness, that confesses but does not repent." - Joan Chittister

The Inextinguishable Blaze

Chapter 13

The Lost Heart of The Church

"We must learn that God is holy. If we are to experience the manifest presence of God's glory, we must repent. When Isaiah saw the glory of God in the Temple, he was driven to brokenness, confession, and repentance. Too many in the West desire to know the manifest love of God without the manifest holiness of God. We have lost the message of repentance."[58]

Throughout this book we have emphasized the importance of thinking right thoughts about God and how thinking wrong thoughts about God is a form of idolatry. The loss of God's holiness in the contemporary Church is a modern idolatry that has caused an entire generation of professing Christians to hold a greatly diminished view of God. As a result, our diminished view of God has produced a generation of "Christian idolaters" - nominal professors and worshipers who, in the words of A.W. Tozer, *"simply imagine things about God and then act as if they were true."*

Our views of God are much like dominoes. Once one falls it becomes nearly impossible to prevent others from falling, too. The loss of any genuine sense or understanding of God's holiness has - in true domino fashion - pushed the Church of our generation into another wrong thought about God. It has produced a God, a Savior and a gospel devoid of repentance. When the consuming fire of God's presence and holiness disappeared from the Church, so did repentance.

---

[58]Sammy Tippit, *Fire in Your Heart: A Call to Personal Holiness* (Moody Press: Chicago, 1987)

The Inextinguishable Blaze

Recovering The Foundations

"If the foundations are destroyed, what shall the righteous do?" Psalm 11:3

The ancient Hebrew Psalmist understood something that we have forgotten. Certain things are "foundational." A truth is "foundational" if its removal jeopardizes whatever you are seeking to build. In the first section of this book we examined the foundational truth of God's holiness. In the

"Our views of God are much like dominoes. Once one falls it becomes nearly impossible to prevent others from falling, too."

process we discovered that holiness is that quality of God's essential nature whereby He is totally and completely separated from sin and is singularly devoted to His own glory. At the same time, holiness is that pure, brilliant, beautiful and penetrating light of God's presence which exposes our sin for the terrible rebellion and offense against God it truly is. How terrible is sin? So terrible that the wrath of God Himself is reserved for one thing and one thing only - the punishment of sin. God responds to sin as a personal affront to His holiness. As we saw in Chapter 7 and the Korean Revival of 1907, when the consuming fire of God's holiness manifests among God's people it exposes the full depth and breadth of our sin and forces us to confront another foundational truth - confession and repentance.

In the Church of God, repentance is a foundational truth. Remove it, and the very nature and existence of the Church is threatened. Exactly how foundational is repentance to the biblical message? That's easy. It IS the biblical message. Don't take my word for it. Listen to the words of Jesus (and John the Baptist):

The Lost Heart Of The Church

*"**Repent**, for the kingdom of heaven is at hand."*
(Matthew 3:2; 4:17; Mark 1:14-15)

The unsettling thing about Jesus' message of repentance is that He directed it at the believers of His day - Jews - the very people whom the Old Testament Scriptures named as God's chosen people. If God's chosen people in Jesus' day were in need of repentance, what makes us think that His people today - the Church - are somehow exempt from that same message?

Unfortunately, repentance has become "the lost heart" of the Church today. There is a reason for this moral and spiritual catastrophe. When the consuming fire of God's presence and holiness disappeared from the message and the life of contemporary "seeker-friendly" Christianity, so did repentance. Now, in the contemporary Evangelical Churches of the early 21st Century, one seldom hears messages on the need for personal or corporate repentance from sin. And yet, when we look at the New testament there are some 58 references to the need to repent. After the command to "listen," the command to "repent" is the most frequent instruction given by the risen Christ to the seven Churches of Asia in Revelation Chapters 2 - 3. Biblically speaking, repentance is a matter close to God's heart.

> *"In the Church of God, repentance is a foundational truth. Remove it, and the very nature and existence of the Church is threatened."*

On That Day . . .

When you and I stand before God on the Day of Judgment, a day which is now closer than when we first believed, He will not ask you to give an account for anyone's sin but your own. That sin or issue in your neighbor's life, which you thought was so terrible and cried out for repentance on their part, will not even come up in the conversation. But God will ask you to explain the log in your own eye, which you steadfastly denied was there and which you stubbornly refused to confess and to repent over. Repentance isn't about any one else. It is about you. It isn't about anyone else's sin. It's about yours. It isn't about what you might think God wants to do in anyone else's life. It's about what God wants to do in your life. It isn't even primarily about the Church calling the world to repent of its sin. It's about the Church seeking to be holy like our God whose presence and holiness are "a consuming fire." It's about living out an authentic life of genuine humility and obedience before a watching world, which has yet to see a genuine role model of repentance, forgiveness and obedience. Perhaps the world will consider the claims of Christ more seriously when it sees the professing Church living out a life of humility, forgiveness and holiness more fully.

A Simple But Profound Question

I am convinced that it is the plan of God for His Church - prior to the soon return of Christ - to bring the Church into a season of profound spiritual outpouring and divine visitation in fulfillment of Isaiah 64:1. God will, indeed, rend the heavens and come down. As God prepares His people for this season of spiritual outpouring He will confront us individually and corporately with a very simple but profound question. Your answer to this question will have a profound effect upon you, your family, your church and your community. Your answer will determine your usefulness in God's hands during the coming revival:

What do you want God to do in your life, the life of your

The Lost Heart Of The Church

family, the life of your church and the life of your community; and what price are you willing to pay to see Him do that?

This question has confronted the people of God at the outset of every historic move of God's Spirit in revival. It was the question which confronted the Church as it stood on the eve of revival in 1857. How do we know? Because they told us so in their own words. Here is what the leadership of the Presbyterian Church said in their official record, written 6 months prior to the outbreak of the great Prayer Revival of 1857.

*"Another and the last evidence, that we cite, of an increasing vigor and efficiency in our denomination is, the intense longing, breathed through all the Narratives for a general, glorious outpouring of the Spirit. The past year has not been one which may be characterized as a year of revivals, although many churches in many Presbyteries have been greatly quickened, and some have been favored with spiritual influences of extraordinary power. . . . This longing for revivals we cannot but consider a cheering indication of the noblest life. Next to a state of actual revival is the sense of its need, and the struggle to attain it at **any sacrifice of treasure, toil or time**.* [59]

The Inextinguishable Blaze

It is time for the Church of our generation to address that question which has confronted the Church throughout history prior to seasons of genuine revival: Are we prepared to "pay the price" that God is laying before us for spiritual awakening

---

[59]***Minutes of the General Assembly of the Presbyterian Church in the United States of America with an Appendix***, 1857, page 418.

The Inextinguishable Blaze

and renewal? The price begins with our willingness to pursue and embrace *"the Inextinguishable Blaze"* of His holiness. It continues with our willingness to embrace the fire of personal and corporate confession and repentance from sin?

The challenge confronting the Church of our generation is simple but profound. Are we willing to seek God on His terms, to pay the price of becoming "children of the burning heart" and carriers of His "inextinguishable blaze"? Are we? Are you? The future of the Church and your role in the coming move of God's Spirit will depend upon your answer.

Chapter 14

Understanding Biblical Repentance

"Then I said, 'Woe is me, for I am ruined! Because I am a man of unclean lips, And I live among a people of unclean lips; For my eyes have seen the King, the Lord of hosts.'" (Isaiah 6:5)

Knowledge and understanding concerning God and His dealings with us are cumulative over time and experience. For this reason I want to build on what we have learned so far in our exploration of God's holiness by offering an experiential-but-biblical definition of repentance. In its essence, *repentance is the response of the human heart to a genuine encounter with the God Whose presence and holiness are "a consuming fire."*

The fiery brilliance of God's holiness exposes our sin for what it truly is, leaving us no "fig leaf" of self-righteousness behind which to hide. No one had to tell Isaiah to repent. Standing in the temple surrounded by the piercing brilliance of this God Who is *"holy, holy, holy,"* repentance was Isaiah's immediate response and his only option. Isaiah's declaration of *"Woe is me, for I am ruined!"* summarizes and describes the responses of men throughout the ages when confronted with the holiness of God.

Earlier in Chapter 7 we read William Newton Blair's description of the Korean Revival of 1907. Another description of that same event comes from an Englishman, Lord William Cecil, who was also present during that visitation. He was so excited and moved by what he witnessed that he did what an Englishman always does when excited; he wrote a letter to ***The Times*** of London, describing the scene:

The Inextinguishable Blaze

.” . . an elder arose and confessed a grudge against a missionary colleague and asked for forgiveness. The missionary stood to pray but reached only the address to Deity: 'Aboji!' 'Father!' when, with a rush, a power from without seemed to take hold of the meeting. The Europeans described its manifestations as terrifying. Nearly everyone present was seized with the most poignant sense of mental anguish; before each one, his sins seemed to be rising in condemnation of his life. Some were springing to their feet, and pleading for an opportunity to relieve their consciences by making their abasement known; and others were silent, but rent with agony, clenching their fists and striking their heads against the ground in the struggle to resist the Power that was forcing them painfully and agonizingly to confess their misdeeds." [60]

Here we have an authentic and historic snapshot of the Church experiencing both the holiness of God and the repentance which it brings about. This is raw, genuine repentance, the response of the human heart to a personal encounter with the God Who is *"holy, holy, holy."* The current absence of any meaningful repentance in the Church today simply reflects our lack of any genuine encounter with the God who is *"holy, holy, holy"* When the contemporary Church lost the fire of God's presence and holiness, it also lost any sense of its need for repentance. As a result of this "idolatry" the Church has experienced a two-fold catastrophe. First, it has lost any sense of its own fallen-ness. Second, it has lost the only God-appointed means for dealing with sin, namely, confession and repentance.

---

[60]J. Edwin Orr, *Evangelical Awakenings In Eastern Asia* (Minneapolis: Bethany Fellowship, Inc., 1975), page 28.

Understanding Biblical Repentance

Repentance In The Old Testament

By the time John the Baptist came preaching a message of repentance in the Gospels, every Jew who heard that message understood what it meant. Why? Because repentance - or the lack of repentance - had played a critical role in the national life of God's people. The message of repentance had been at the heart of the messages of the Old Testament Prophets. Through the preaching ministry of the Old Testament Prophets, The Holy One of Israel continually confronted His wayward people with His holiness while calling them to repent of their sins and disobedience and return to Him. In 721 B.C. the Northern Kingdom of Israel perished at the hands of the Assyrians for their sins and their refusal to repent. 135 years later, in 586 B.C., the Southern Kingdom of Judah fell to the Babylonians and was taken into Captivity for their refusal to respond to the prophetic call of God to repent delivered through the prophet Jeremiah. The people of God in the Old Testament understood well what repentance meant. They had simply chosen to NOT obey, and had paid a high price for their disobedience (See Chapter 15 below, *"And Then They Repented"*).

The concept of repentance in the life of God's Old Testament people was most often expressed by the use of two Hebrew words. The first Hebrew word for repentance (*nacham*) originally meant *"to draw the breath forcibly, to pant or to groan."* Over time it came to mean *"to be sorry, to pity, to grieve"* and then *"to feel repentance"* or *"to repent."* Essentially, *nacham* describes a "grieving" which produces a change of attitude, heart or disposition, a change of mind, a change of purpose, or a change of one's conduct.

The second Hebrew word for repentance (*shuwb*) carries the basic meaning of *"movement back to the point of departure."* *Shuwb* literally means *"to turn and go in a different direction."*

The Inextinguishable Blaze

Shuwb is the twelfth most frequently used Hebrew verb in the OT. It occurs 1,060 times, with an additional eight times in biblical Aramaic (where it is spelled *tuwb*). The word is used for simple physical motion about 270 times. *Shuwb* occurs most often in the book of Jeremiah (111 times) where it serves as Jeremiah's favorite word for repentance.

Let's take a look at an example of these two words being used together in a way which highlights their unique meanings:

*"Now it came about when Pharaoh had let the people go, that God did not lead them by the way of the land of the Philistines, even though it was near; for God said, 'Lest the people **change their minds** when they see war, and they **return** to Egypt.'"* (Exodus 13:17)

The experience of Israel coming out of Egypt gives us a practical demonstration of these two words, namely, a profound "change of heart" (*nacham*) followed by an equally profound "turning" which results in a change in direction (*shuwb*). The context is the Exodus from Egypt. The Hebrew people had been slaves in Egypt for some 400 years. Now they were leaving Egypt on their way to the Promised Land. But they were unprepared for the prospect of battle or war. So, God led them in such a way (basically He took them "the long way around") as to avoid war. Why? Because God knew that the difficulties of a battle might cause the people to grieve and have a "change of heart" about the whole deal, causing them to abandon their purpose and literally "turn around" and go back to Egypt. This incident gives us a basic practical explanation of two aspects of all genuine repentance. Biblically speaking, repentance consists of a change of heart, mind or purpose which results in a profound "turning"; a profound change of direction or behavior.

Understanding Biblical Repentance

While the technical vocabulary of repentance is absent, we can see the two-fold nature of repentance at work in the experience of Isaiah (which we treated in depth earlier in Chapter 11). Isaiah's encounter with the God Who is *"holy, holy, holy"* resulted in a profound "change of mind" regarding Who God was and who Isaiah was in relation to God, summed up in the phrase *"Woe is me, for I am ruined!"* He was indeed "ruined," in ways even Isaiah probably didn't realize. His perception and understanding of God was forever changed. From that day forward Isaiah would always see God as *"The Holy One of Israel."* But Isaiah's encounter with the God Who is *"holy, holy, holy"* also resulted in a profound "turning." Isaiah experienced a profound "change of direction or behavior," summed up in the words, *"Then I said, 'Here am I. Send me!'"* Isaiah's encounter with God was so profound that he announced his willingness to "go" without even asking God where he would be going. No negotiating. Just obedience. And that's profound repentance.

Repentance In The New Testament

Everything we have discovered and learned in the Old Testament regarding repentance now carries over to the New Testament. Repentance is expressed in the Greek word *metanoia*, which literally meant to have an "after thought" or a "change of mind," resulting in a change of direction or action.

Repentance In The Ministry of John the Baptist - John the Baptist was the "forerunner" whose ministry prepared the way for the coming of Jesus. A call to personal repentance for the forgiveness of sins and to *"flee the wrath to come"* defined both the message and the ministry of John the Baptist, *"And he went into all the region around the Jordan, proclaiming a baptism of repentance for the forgiveness of sins"* (Luke 3:3; see also Matthew 3:1-11; Mark 1:4; and

The Inextinguishable Blaze

Luke 3:1-18).

Repentance In The Ministry of Jesus - Jesus began His public ministry by proclaiming a public call to repent, *"The time is fulfilled, and the kingdom of God is at hand; repent and believe in the gospel."* (Mark 1:15; see also Matthew 4:17). Jesus denounced cities where He had performed many miracles but where the people had failed to repent (Matthew 11:20). He defined His own ministry in terms of repentance when He told the Pharisees (and His disciples), *"I have not come to call the righteous but sinners to repentance"* (Luke 5:32). It is clear from Mark's account of the commissioning and sending out of the disciples that Jesus instructed them to proclaim repentance as part of their public message, *"So they went out and proclaimed that people should repent"* (Mark 6:12). He twice warned the crowds who followed Him that they would perish *"unless you repent"* (Luke 13:3 & 5). Jesus emphasized both the message and the importance of repentance when He told His disciples that there was rejoicing in heaven whenever a sinner repented (Luke 15:7). That Jesus regarded repentance as central to the message which the Church would preach after He was gone is clear from His last words to His disciples in Luke 24:

"Then he opened their minds to understand the Scriptures, and said to them, 'Thus it is written, that the Christ should suffer and on the third day rise from the dead, and that repentance and forgiveness of sins should be proclaimed in his name to all nations, beginning from Jerusalem. You are witnesses of these things.'" (Luke 24:44-48)

Jesus As "Holiness Incarnate." Christians today like to think and talk about Jesus as "love incarnate." We preach messages, sing songs and write books about Jesus being

Understanding Biblical Repentance

"love incarnate." And that is true. Jesus IS love incarnate. But it is even MORE true that Jesus is "holiness incarnate." Through His incarnation Jesus lived a life that manifested God's holiness and demanded a response

"the holiness of Jesus is so majestic that religious people can't stand it, except in small doses, and then only at a distance."

of repentance on the part of all who came in contact with Him, including the religious leaders of His day. Pastor and theologian R.C. Sproul describes it this way:

"The presence of Jesus represented the presence of the genuine in the midst of the bogus. Here authentic holiness appeared; the counterfeiters of holiness were not pleased . . . . Holiness provokes hatred. The greater the holiness, the greater the human hostility toward it. It seems insane. No man was ever more loving than Jesus Christ. Yet even His love made people angry. His love was a perfect love, a transcendent and holy love, but His very love brought trauma to people. This kind of love is so majestic we can't stand it . . . . So it was with Christ. The world could tolerate Jesus; they could love Him, but only at a distance. Christ is safe for us if securely bound by space and time. But a present Christ could not survive in a world of hostile men. It was the judgment of Caiaphas that, for the good of the nation, Jesus must die."[61]

As "holiness incarnate" Jesus confronted religious people with a form of God's holiness that threatened their self-made holiness and called their religion-shaped spirituality into

_____

[61]R.C. Sproul, **The Holiness of God** (Grand Rapids: Tyndale House Publishers, 2nd Edition, 2000). pp. 64-71.

question. His life as "holiness incarnate" presented an on-going demand for repentance. He continues to do the same thing today. To paraphrase Dr. Sproul's observation, the holiness of Jesus is so majestic that religious people can't stand it, except in small doses, and then only at a distance. In Jesus religious people find no rest from the message of "holiness incarnate": *"Repent, and follow me."*

Repentance In The Ministry of the Early Church - Repentance stood at the heart of the gospel proclaimed by the early church. Repentance from sin was the "punch line" of Peter's three sermons: to the crowd on the Day of Pentecost, to the crowd gathered at the Gate Beautiful, and to the Council of religious leaders.

"And Peter said to them, 'Repent and be baptized every one of you in the name of Jesus Christ for the forgiveness of your sins, and you will receive the gift of the Holy Spirit'" (Acts 2:38).

"Repent therefore, and turn again, that your sins may be blotted out, that times of refreshing may come from the presence of the Lord, and that he may send the Christ appointed for you, Jesus, whom heaven must receive until the time for restoring all the things about which God spoke by the mouth of his holy prophets long ago" (Acts 3:19-21).

"God exalted him at his right hand as Leader and Savior, to give repentance to Israel and forgiveness of sins" (Acts 5:31).

But Peter was not alone in his emphasis on repentance. The Church elders in Acts 11 recognized the importance of repentance in bringing eternal life to the Gentiles following Peter's proclamation of the gospel to the Gentile, Cornelius, and his family, *"When they heard these things they fell silent. And they glorified God, saying, 'Then to the Gentiles also*

Understanding Biblical Repentance

God has granted repentance that leads to life'" (Acts 11:18). Furthermore, the writer of the Epistle to the Hebrews includes repentance in a list of six key issues ("elementary teachings about Christ") which the early church regarded as necessary for believers to understand in order to be grounded and prepared to "press on to maturity":

"Therefore leaving the elementary teaching about the Christ, let us press on to maturity, not laying again a foundation of repentance from dead works and of faith toward God, of instruction about washings, and laying on of hands, and the resurrection of the dead, and eternal judgment. And this we shall do, if God permits." (Hebrews 6:1-3)

Repentance In The Ministry of Paul - It is quickly evident that the gospel which Paul proclaimed was the same gospel that Jesus, the disciples and the early church all proclaimed - a gospel of repentance from sin. When preaching to Greek philosophers on Mars Hill Paul proclaimed, *"The times of ignorance God overlooked, but now he commands all people everywhere to repent, because he has fixed a day on which he will judge the world in righteousness by a man whom he has appointed; and of this he has given assurance to all by raising him from the dead"* (Acts 17:30-31). We should note that according to this passage repentance is not an option. It is a command. When he spoke to the Ephesian elders in Acts 20, Paul reminded them that during his three years of ministry in their midst, *"I did not shrink from declaring to you anything that was profitable, and teaching you in public and from house to house, testifying both to Jews and to Greeks of repentance toward God and of faith in our Lord Jesus Christ"* (Acts 20:20-21). And, finally, presenting a defense of his ministry before King Agrippa, Paul summarized his message to the Gentiles as follows: *"that they should repent and turn to God, performing deeds in keeping with their repentance"* (Acts 26:20).

The Inextinguishable Blaze

Repentance And The Seven Churches of Asia - As we have noted on previous occasions, next to the command to "listen" (literally, *"He who has an ear, let him hear"*), the most frequent command of the Risen Christ to the Seven Churches of Asia is the command to "repent." [62] What is particularly noteworthy here is that all of the admonitions to repent that are directed to five of the seven Churches are directed to Christians, not to unbelievers. This is important because part of the present misunderstanding of repentance in the contemporary Church is that repentance is a message that only applies to unbelievers. Christians are somehow exempt from any need to repent. I have had mature Christian leaders (i.e., people who should know better) tell me that they are unaware of any sin in their lives that requires repentance. I try to resist the urge to suggest that they reflect on the sin of spiritual pride. Instead, I point them to the Scriptures and suggest that they reflect on 1 John 1:8-10 which says,

"If we say we have no sin, we deceive ourselves, and the truth is not in us. If we confess our sins, he is faithful and just to forgive us our sins and to cleanse us from all unrighteousness. If we say we have not sinned, we make him a liar, and his word is not in us."

We should remember that the Christians of the five Churches that Jesus rebuked and called to repentance in Revelation 2 - 3 didn't know they were in trouble until Jesus pointed out their sins and commanded them to repent. Did the Ephesian Christians know that they were guilty of abandoning their first

---

[62]Se our book, ***When Jesus Visit's His Church: A Study Of The Seven Church Of Asia, available through our website from Amazon.*** The word "repent" occurs 8 times in 7 verses and 5 Churches: See Revelation 2:5; 2:16; 2:21; 2:22; 3:3; 3:19.

Understanding Biblical Repentance

love and substituting religious busyness for spiritual intimacy before Jesus confronted them about it? Did the believers in the Church at Pergamum know they were a compromised Church before the Risen Christ presented them with a choice between the double-edged sword of his mouth or the sword of the Emperor, and called them to repent? Did the believers in Sardis understand that they were spiritually dead, that the oil of the Holy Spirit was gone from their lamps and that they were living on a reputation that was no longer true? Did they know it before Jesus pointed it out and called them to repent? And did the Christians of Laodicea know they had lost their zeal, had become lukewarm and that Jesus was preparing to spit them out of His mouth before He confronted them and commanded them to *"be zealous and repent"*?

The messages to The Seven Churches of Asia are instructive. They teach us that an unrepentant Church - a Church unaware of its own spiritual condition and its need for repentance - is a Church where the consuming fire of God's presence and holiness has gone out. Does this describe you? Does it describe your Church?

The Inextinguishable Blaze

It is time for the Church to recover "the lost heart" of repentance. The absence of genuine repentance in the Church of our generation betrays the lack of a genuine encounter with the God Whose presence and holiness *are "a consuming fire."* When you or I or the Church lose our sense of God's holiness in our midst, it isn't long before the fire goes out on the altar of our hearts. We soon become complacent and self-satisfied, and repentance as a message and a lifestyle disappears. God earnestly desires a people who will repent by turning away from anything that separates us from a deeper walk with Him, and which compromises our witness and testimony to the world.

The Inextinguishable Blaze

Chapter 15

And Then They Repented

"In the eighth month of the second year of Darius, the word of the Lord came to Zechariah the prophet, the son of Berechiah, the son of Iddo saying, 'The Lord was very angry with your fathers. Therefore say to them, 'Thus says the Lord of hosts, 'Return to Me,' declares the Lord of hosts, 'that I may return to you,' says the Lord of hosts. 'Do not be like your fathers, to whom the former prophets proclaimed, saying, 'Thus says the Lord of hosts, 'Return now from your evil ways and from your evil deeds.' But they did not listen or give heed to Me,' declares the Lord. 'Your fathers, where are they? And the prophets, do they live forever? 'But did not My words and My statutes, which I commanded My servants the prophets, overtake your fathers? Then they repented and said, 'As the Lord of hosts purposed to do to us in accordance with our ways and our deeds, so He has dealt with us.'" (Zechariah 1:1-6)

An Examination of Zechariah 1:1-6

Over the years I have taught that there are two ways to do the will of God. We can do the will of God voluntarily (what I call "the easy way"), or we can do the will of God involuntarily (what I call "the hard way"). The people of Zechariah's day chose to do God's will involuntarily (yep, the hard way), and therein lies a story of repentance delayed, but not denied.

Our story actually begins some 70 years earlier, prior to the Babylonian captivity. Josiah reigned as King over the Southern Kingdom of Judah (think Jerusalem and its extended suburbs) and the prophet Jeremiah ministered God's word. Josiah was a good King who led the nation through a period of national revival and reformation. But it was a river wide and shallow. The hearts of the people

The Inextinguishable Blaze

remained essentially unchanged, and through the ministry of the Prophet Jeremiah God called the people to turn away from their spiritual adultery. He called them to repent. Repentance, both personal and corporate, stands out as one of the great recurring themes of the book of Jeremiah (The Hebrew word for repent occurs some 112 times in 92 verses). Judgment was coming, God declared, but there was still time to repent.

But it was not to be. The false prophets of peace and prosperity found a receptive and willing audience. Their fifteen minutes of fame coincided with Judah's last fifteen minutes of national life before disaster. Politicians with too much to lose, priests who should have known better and people who were comfortable in their spiritual adulteries all turned a deaf ear to God's call of repentance and took their anger out on Jeremiah. The few remaining years of national existence quickly clicked by, the judgment of God fell and the Kingdom of Judah was carried away to Babylon and captivity, just as God - through Jeremiah - had promised.

Now, fast forward 70 years. The Babylonian captivity has ended and the people of God are once again returning to Jerusalem. Zechariah (along with his contemporary, Haggai) is ministering to the returnees and he opens his ministry with a spiritual history lesson (always a crowd pleaser!), which we find in Zechariah 1:1-6. Whether or not Zechariah meant to offer five points and a punch line, we'll never know. But it works for me, so here goes. Zechariah wanted the people of Jerusalem to grasp five important historical/spiritual truths:

1. First, Zechariah wanted them to understand God's anger toward their fathers for their sin and disobedience. *"The Lord was very angry with your fathers."* The Babylonian Captivity hadn't been an accident of history, or the result of Judah's military ineptitude before a greatly superior enemy. It had been the sovereign act of God in judgment and punishment for their unrepented sin, the express consequence of both their actions and inactions. They had sown the wind, and had reaped the whirlwind, just as God had promised so many years before.

2. Second, Zechariah wanted to remind them of God's original command to their fathers to repent. *"Therefore say to them, 'Thus says the Lord of hosts, 'Return to Me,' declares the Lord of hosts, 'that I may return to you,' says the Lord of hosts."* In a mere word and a moment's time Zechariah reminded them of Jeremiah's ministry to their fathers. There were probably old men in Zechariah's audience who, as children in Jerusalem, had personally heard Jeremiah deliver God's message of pending judgment and personal repentance (the Hebrew word translated "return" in Zechariah is also Jeremiah's favorite Hebrew word for "repent"). Old men heard old words with old ears, but with new understanding, as did their children.

3. Third, Zechariah wanted to pass along God's fresh admonishment to His people. *"Do not be like your fathers, to whom the former prophets proclaimed, saying, 'Thus says the Lord of hosts, 'Return now from your evil ways and from your evil deeds.' But they did not listen or give heed to Me,' declares the Lord."* Zechariah was building a lesson here by translating a past disaster of disobedience into a present opportunity for obedience and blessing. Learn from the past. Don't be like your fathers, who heard the word of repentance but *"did not listen or give heed."* There was an unspoken question hanging in the air, *"Would the new generation of the children learn from the experience of their fathers?"* Only time would tell.

4. Fourth, Zechariah wanted them to understand God's persistence. *"Your fathers, where are they? And the*

The Inextinguishable Blaze

prophets, do they live forever? 'But did not My words and My statutes, which I commanded My servants the prophets, overtake your fathers?'" To put this in contemporary terms, the people of God

"When God calls a man or a people to repent, the call of God will always outlast the man, or the people."

had been "overtaken" by *"the hound of heaven,"* Who pursues the object of His eternal desire with a relentless love. The word of repentance proclaimed by Jeremiah had not been received, but neither had it "gone away." When God calls a man or a people to repent, the call of God will always outlast the man, or the people. God's call of repentance to the fathers had been rejected, yet it remained. The people thought their refusal was the "last word." But God's word is always the last word. God's word overtook the fathers. When did that take place? In the Babylonian Captivity. God's word of repentance had not evaporated into the spiritual ether. Rather it had moved from the "easy" stage (when they could have repented rather easily and voluntarily) into the "hard" stage, when their repentance would come harder (even "involuntarily") and at a much higher price. The word of repentance, which had been delivered and rejected during days of heady arrogance and seemingly clear skies, had "overtaken" them in dark and stormy days of disaster, calamity and captivity.

5. Fifth, Zechariah wanted them to grasp God's unfailing purpose, namely, to bring His people to renewed repentance and faith. *"Then they repented and said, 'As the Lord of hosts purposed to do to us in accordance with our ways and our deeds, so He has dealt with us.'"* It must have been an uncomfortable dawning, a bitter realization that God had indeed accomplished His purpose which He had declared so many years before. At some unspecified point during the

And Then They Repented

Babylonian Captivity the fathers had repented and acknowledged that everything which had happened to them was simply the deserved consequences of God dealing with them *"in accordance with our ways and our deeds."* That had to hurt, and it certainly left a mark.

Conclusion: Zechariah's point in this spiritual history lesson was really quite simple: The fathers who had heard God's call to repentance, who had experienced God's judgment and who had eventually repented, had also discovered that there are two ways to do the will of God: voluntarily (that would be the easy way) or involuntarily (that would be the hard way). Their fathers could have repented 70 years earlier, and like all such missed opportunities, we can only guess what the results of that repentance might have been. But they eventually did repent, and that is the prolonged point of this story.

Repentance Then and Now

Some things haven't really changed in 2,500 years. Repentance remains an unpopular message, even today, whether among the seeker friendly masses who want their best life now (*sans* repentance), or among complacent contemporary Christians who think that repentance is something reserved for "really bad people": pedophiles, chainsaw murders or worse . . . like politicians from the other party.

As a result, in the contemporary church repentance has, for the most part, suffered twin fates. On the one hand, it has itself been purposely driven out of seeker friendly churches like an unwelcome demon. After all, to call men (and women) to repent and shun those deeds of the flesh which they love and to embrace those godly virtues which our old un-repentant nature despises is, well, uncool. Not exactly a

The Inextinguishable Blaze

congregation builder, according to the best church growth manuals. On the other hand, repentance has suffered the ignominious fate of respectability and "Christian-political-correctness" in "repentance events." Make believe leaders practice "representational repentance" with other make believe leaders whom they have never met, much less sinned against. Together they shed pseudo-tears as they lead pseudo-penitents through the formalized steps of pseudo-repentance in the hope that the pseudo-deities of their imagination will be somehow pleased with their pseudo-offerings.[63]

Welcome to therapy (*the whole experience made me feel so much better*) masquerading as repentance.

You may think I am over-reaching my point, but such formalized and empty spiritual exercises are not new. They were taking place in Jeremiah's day, too. How do I know that? Because he says so, *"So the Lord said to me, 'Do not pray for the welfare of this people. When they fast, I am not going to listen to their cry; and when they offer burnt offering and grain offering, I am not going to accept them. Rather I am going to make an end of them by the sword, famine and pestilence."* (Jeremiah 14:11-12) Biblical fasting is a

---

[63]To witness and reflect on such performances is to suddenly realize that the mistake of the people of God in Jeremiah's day was not their failure to repent of their spiritual adultery and idolatry. Apparently, their real mistake was their failure to find a Canaanite (or a Phoenician, since they are related) and to formally repent to them and ask forgiveness for their Jewish ancestors having slaughtered their Phoenician ancestors and stealing their land. This, of course could have opened the door to a virtually limitless cottage industry, since the same procedure could be practiced on behalf of the Hivites, the Hittites, the Perizzites, the Girgshites, the Kenites, the Jebusites, the Amorites and "every-other-ite" between Egypt and Mesopotamia. The potential for repentance events, books, CDs and DVDs would have been endless . . . but, alas, I digress.

And Then They Repented

God-appointed means of expressing personal repentance, as well as a personal act of sacrificial worship (i.e., worship which costs us something). But the people of Jeremiah's day had reached a point where they went through the motions without the heart or the spirit. They outwardly fasted - went through the religious motions - but did not genuinely repent or worship. And to fast without genuinely repenting is like praying without ever talking to God. Don't bother, because God isn't in it. It is "religious therapy" masquerading as genuine prayer and repentance. For this reason alone it is not surprising that God specifically instructed Jeremiah (15:19-21) to practice a lifestyle of genuine personal repentance before Him. Only then would God restore him, cause him to stand before Him, teach him to *"extract the precious from the worthless"* (i.e., exercise discernment) and enable Him to truly become "My spokesperson."

Like Jeremiah, any man or woman living a lifestyle of authentic personal repentance amidst a church absorbed with "therapy sideshows" will quickly find themselves standing as *"a fortified wall of bronze"* in an age of spiritual and moral mud huts.

My view of repentance is the same as my view of sin: I prefer the real thing over any imitation or substitute. I find it difficult, to the point of incredulity, to believe that we have so few personal, real and immediate sins in need of confession and repentance that we must dig up dead ancestors and repent for them. Any good Mormon must be thoroughly confused at this point. They baptize for their dead ancestors (hence, their profound interest in genealogy). We merely repent for ours. I doubt a good Mormon understands the theological difference . . . and I doubt that most good evangelicals could begin to explain it to them.

It was John Donne (1572-1631), the English poet and pastor

The Inextinguishable Blaze

who wrote,

"No man is an island, entire of itself; every man is a piece of the continent, a part of the main; if a clod be washed away by the sea, Europe is the less, as well as if a promontory were, as well as if a manor of thy friends or of thine own were; any man's death diminishes me, because I am involved in mankind; and therefore never send to know for whom the bell tolls; it tolls for thee."

Do you get his point, and do you understand its relationship to genuine repentance? I have a vested interest in your repentance . . . and you have a vested interest in mine. Why? Because, as believers, we share a common life in the body of Christ (see 1 Corinthians 12-14). Like the believers gathering together in the Seven Churches of Asia, we share a common fate as the Risen Christ chastens, disciplines and cleanses His Church. As the Holy Spirit begins to "toll the bell" of repentance in the Church, do not *"send to know for whom the bell tolls; it tolls for thee."*

The Inextinguishable Blaze

It is time for the Church of God abandon its love affair with "therapy" and to embrace *"the Inextinguishable Blaze"* of genuine repentance. The absence of genuine repentance in the contemporary Church is a tell-tale sign that *"the Inextinguishable Blaze"* of God's presence is absent. The true fire of God's holiness has gone out, replaced by the false fire of "therapy" and pseudo-repentance.

And our inability to discern the difference has become our judgment.

Chapter 16

Repentance And Revival

"I have a word for you from God."

On Monday, October 31, 1904 a 26 year old former coal miner and first-semester bible school student named Evan Roberts boarded a train for the ride home to the town of Loughor, Wales (roughly eight miles outside of Swansea). His return home was unexpected and caught his family by surprise. His mother thought that maybe he had been preaching somewhere on Sunday and was stopping by home on his way back to school. But Roberts explained that he was home for the week, that he had experienced a profound encounter with God, and that he had come home to lead the young people of his home church (the Moriah Calvinstic Methodist Church) in some meetings which he believed would be the beginning of a great revival. Two days later, on Wednesday evening of that first week home, Roberts spoke at the Libanus Calvinistic Methodist Church in the near-by village of Gorseinon. After the official meeting closed, Roberts led a group back to the Moriah church for an "after meeting." There Evan Roberts declared, *"I have a word for you from God,"* and proceeded to challenge his audience with the following four points:

1. You must confess any known sin to God, and put any wrong done to man right;
2. You must put away any doubtful habit;
3. You must obey the Spirit promptly;
4. You must confess your faith in Christ publicly.

Welcome to holiness, repentance and intimacy as it found practical expression during a profound season of spiritual awakening and revival. Points one and two express the concepts of holiness and repentance. The fire of God's

The Inextinguishable Blaze

holiness forces us to confront our sin and to deal with it through confession and repentance. Points three and four express the concept of intimacy with God. It is impossible to have intimacy with God if we are unwilling to obey the prompting of His Spirit, or to openly confess our relationship with Him before men. These "Four Points" played a prominent role in nearly every meeting Evan Roberts conducted for the next 18 months of his revival work as *"the Inextinguishable Blaze"* of God's Presence and holiness burned its way through the Church and across Wales.

The Role of Repentance Revival

During the 1830s and 40s the most prominent evangelist in America was Charles Grandison Finney. On one occasion in 1826 Finney was preaching in the area of Utica, New York when he was invited by his brother-in-law to visit and tour a local cotton factory where he was the Superintendent. When Finney arrived at the factory he proceeded to walk across the factory floor to meet his brother-in-law. As he passed through the factory workers on the factory floor began to weep. Soon, many of the workers were weeping and unable to work. The factory owner was not a Christian. But when he realized what was happening he closed the factory, saying *"Stop the mill and let the people attend to religion; for it is more important that our souls should be saved than that this factory run."* He then invited Finney to preach to the assembled workers. Finney preached, and over the course of the week that followed nearly every worker in the factory professed Christ as savior.[64]

---

[64] You'll find Finney's account of this story on page 183 in his memoirs.

Repentance And Revival

Historic seasons of spiritual awakening and revival - like the two described above - represent times when God Himself sovereignly moved as "a consuming fire" in the midst of His people. The consuming fire of God's presence and holiness among His people

> *"A genuine revival without genuine personal repentance is a contradiction in terms, like lukewarm fire, or fire on ice."*

causes widespread confession and repentance from sin as the fire of God burns its way through the Church (see our earlier accounts of the Korean Revival of 1907). A genuine revival without genuine personal repentance is a contradiction in terms, like lukewarm fire, or fire on ice.

The importance of repentance in true revival cannot be overstated. Not only is repentance the response of the human heart to a genuine encounter with the God Whose presence and holiness are "a consuming fire," repentance is to revival what roots are to a tree. A tall tree with shallow roots is a disaster waiting to happen. When the winds of adversity blow, tall trees with shallow roots are easily blown over with disastrous results. Much of the Church today resembles a spiritual tree with shallow roots. Our generation has never been forced by adversity or persecution to dig its spiritual roots deep into God's Presence. We have created entire theologies of "blessing and prosperity" to avoid such unpleasant experiences and to convince others that they can avoid it, too. The result is a generation of trees with shallow roots. To use a biblical description, we have sown seed on rocky ground and among thorns. It has sprouted up, but it is unprepared for tribulation, for persecution, or for resisting the deceitfulness of riches. Why, then, are we surprised by the lack of fruit? We have achieved the very results Jesus warned us would arise from the very things we are doing:

The Inextinguishable Blaze

"As for what was sown on rocky ground, this is the one who hears the word and immediately receives it with joy, yet he has no root in himself, but endures for a while, and when tribulation or persecution arises on account of the word, immediately he falls away. As for what was sown among thorns, this is the one who hears the word, but the cares of the world and the deceitfulness of riches choke the word, and it proves unfruitful." (Matthew 13:20-22)

The relevant question for the Church of our generation is both simple and profound: Are we willing to take the first steps toward God in repentance, asking Him to meet us in this process and to reveal to us our own spiritual blindness, poverty and need. I am reminded of Paul's words to Timothy when he said, *"And the Lord's bond-servant must not be quarrelsome, but be kind to all, able to teach, patient when wronged, with gentleness correcting those who are in opposition, if perhaps <u>God may grant them repentance</u> leading to the knowledge of the truth . ."* (2 Timothy 2:25).

Our goal in pursuing the fire of God's holiness and the repentance which that fire produces is NOT to artificially create something to repent over. Rather, our goal is to ask God Himself to grant to each of us a genuine spirit of repentance that expresses the heart of God and the spiritual need of our own lives. Paul talks in this verse about *"repentance toward God."* This is a reminder that our lives as Christians must never be defined by what we are against. Our spiritual lives must ultimately be defined by what we turn towards. Repentance is more than turning away from sin. It also involves a profound turning towards God. Repentance is saying "no" both to sin as God reveals it and to anything which separates us from a deeper walk with God, and saying "yes" to greater intimacy with Him. And that is a good thing.

Repentance And Revival

Repenting For Our Poor Testimony

One of my favorite Christian thinkers during my college days was Os Guinness. His book, *The Dust of Death*, a critique of the collapse of western thought, was required reading among Christian college students during the 1970s (It is still an excellent read). Guinness studied under Dr. Francis Schaeffer at L'Abri and Schaeffer's thought resonates through much of Guinness' writings even today. In his book, *The Long Journey Home*, Dr. Guinness discusses the three impediments to Christian faith most often cited by unbelievers. The first impediment is the problem of pain, evil and suffering and how a loving God can allow such things in the world. The second impediment cited is the problem of the historical Jesus, particularly in light of such things as The Jesus Project (which questions the historical veracity of the biblical accounts of Jesus' life). The third impediment to Christian faith cited by unbelievers is . . . . Christians. That's right. When it comes to evangelism and the gospel, we are often our own worst enemy. At least, that's how unbelievers often see us. Sometimes the worst thing we can do for an unbeliever is to bring him or her to Church. What makes us think that the sins of pride, gossip, prejudice, anger, judgmentalism and the like are somehow OK in the life of God's people, but are to be condemned in the life of an unbeliever. And how can we ask and expect unbelievers to repent of those things which separate them from God when God's own people are unwilling to do so?

The Inextinguishable Blaze

It is time for the Church of our generation to embrace the fire of God's holiness and repentance as we earnestly fast and pray for spiritual awakening. It is time for us to acknowledge that genuine repentance and spiritual awakening must begin

The Inextinguishable Blaze

within the Church among those laying claim to faith and holiness. The world will be far more impressed with our preaching and our message when they see the genuineness of our own repentance over our own sins.

Chapter 17

Fasting, Repentance And Revival

"And with fasting let us always join in fervent prayer, pouring out our whole souls before God, confessing our sins with all their aggravations, humbling ourselves under his mighty hand, laying open before him all our wants, all our guiltiness and helplessness. This is a season for enlarging our prayers, both in behalf of ourselves and of our brethren. Let us now bewail the sins of our people, and cry aloud for the city of our God: that the Lord may build up Zion, and cause his face to shine on her desolations." - John Wesley

John Wesley, the founder of the Methodist Church, was a highly disciplined person in his personal spiritual devotions. He fasted two days every week, every Wednesday and every Friday, from the time he got up in the morning until after 3:00 in the afternoon. And he refused to appoint to the Methodist ministry any man who would not commit himself to fast two days per week. As one of the leaders of the First Great Awakening in England, Wesley understood the important role fasting plays in confession of sin, genuine personal repentance and spiritual preparation for revival. Indeed, it is safe to say that every historic revival of the past 250 years has been preceded by seasons of fasting and prayer. Take the example of James McGready and the Second Great Awakening on the American frontier.

In January of 1797 the Reverend James McGready, a Presbyterian pastor recently moved from North Carolina, began pastoring three small congregations in Logan County Kentucky situated along three small rivers, the Muddy, the Red, and the Gasper. McGready was an unabashed carrier of *"the Inextinguishable Blaze"* and man given to passionate, biblical preaching, and concerted fasting and prayer. He challenged the members in each of his three congregations

The Inextinguishable Blaze

to enter into a signed covenant and agree to fast and pray regularly for an out-pouring of the Holy Spirit and the conversion of sinners. Here is what the covenant said:

"When we consider the word and promises of a compassionate God, to the poor lost family of Adam, we find the strongest encouragement for Christians to pray in faith - to ask in the name of Jesus for the conversion of their fellow-men. None ever went to Christ, when on earth, with the case of their friends that were denied, and although the days of his humiliation are ended, yet for the encouragement of His people, he has left it on record, that when two or three agree upon earth, to ask in prayer, believing, it shall be done. Again whatsoever ye shall ask the Father in my name that will I do, that the Father may be glorified in the Son. With these promises before us we feel encouraged to unite our supplications to a prayer-hearing God, for the out-pouring of his Spirit, that his people may be quickened and comforted, and that our children, and sinners generally, may be converted. Therefore, we bind ourselves to observe the third Saturday of each month, for one year, as a day of fasting and prayer, for the conversion of sinners in Logan County, and throughout the world. We also engage to spend one-half hour every Saturday evening, beginning at the setting of the sun, and one-half hour every Sabbath morning, at the rising of the sun, in pleading with God to revive His work." [65]

Within a year of McGready and his congregations entering into their fasting and prayer covenant spiritual awakening and revival began breaking out among their churches. That

---

[65]Covenant of Rev. James McGready from James Smith, *History of the Christian Church, Including a History of the Cumberland Presbyterian Church* (1835). Quoted in Catharine C. Cleveland, *The Great Revival In The West 1787-1805*. Copyright 1916 University of Chicago. (Gloucester, Mass: Peter Smith, 1959).

Fasting, Repentance And Revival

revival quickly became the 2nd Great Awakening which burned across the American frontier and transformed the American Southeast into "the Bible Belt." Do we as a Church need anything less than that today?

Fasting And Repentance

We live today among a generation of Christians who, if they fast at all, fast to get things from God. It seems that when the Church lost the heart of repentance, it also lost the heart of fasting. In the swing from a God-centered theology to a man-centered theology fasting became one of the casualties. It lost its role in the pursuit of God, and took on a new role in the pursuit of "things." Allow me to push the pendulum back in the other direction for a moment by suggesting that, in its essence, fasting represents two profound spiritual "acts" toward God. First, genuine fasting represents a profound act of personal sacrificial worship - a worship which "costs" us something. Second, fasting represents a profound act of personal repentance in which we humble ourselves before the throne of grace, confessing our sins and imploring His favor.

On a broader level, biblical fasting has always played an important role in how the people of God - both individually and collectively - have sought God in personal repentance for their sin. They did this in four basic ways.

1. The people of God fasted in order to humble themselves before God. In 1 Peter 5:5-6 Peter exhorts elders to *"clothe yourselves with humility toward one another, for God is opposed to the proud, but gives grace to the humble. Humble yourselves therefore under the mighty hand of God . . ."* Confronting our own sin requires humility on our part, and there is a clear scriptural relationship between humbling ourselves and fasting. In Leviticus 16:31 God

The Inextinguishable Blaze

instructed the Israelites to "afflict" their souls each year on the Day of Atonement. The Hebrew word translated "afflict" in Leviticus 16:31 means *"to be bowed down or afflicted."* It is the same word translated "humble" in Psalm 35:13 where David declared, *"I humbled my soul with fasting."* The same word appears alongside fasting in other passages, such as Ezra 8:21 where Ezra proclaimed a fast, *"that we might humble ourselves."* In Scripture, fasting is God's appointed means for His people to humble themselves. Genuine biblical fasting represents a profound act of personal repentance in which we humble ourselves before the throne of grace.

2. The people of God fasted as a means of confessing their sins. The relationship between fasting and the confession of sin is powerfully demonstrated in Ezra 9:5ff, *"But at the evening offering I arose from my **humiliation**, even with my garment and my robe torn, and I fell on my knees and stretched out my hands to the Lord my God; and I said, 'O my God, I am ashamed and embarrassed to lift up my face to Thee, my God, for our iniquities have risen above our heads, and our guilt has grown even to the heavens.'"*

The Hebrew word translated "humiliation" means *"to afflict or humble oneself by fasting."* [66] The remainder of the chapter records Ezra's confession of the people's sin and his prayer for God's forgiveness. The fire of genuine repentance is contagious. And as a result of Ezra's fasting and confession, a spirit of conviction for sin began to spread among the people, *"Now while Ezra was praying and making confession, weeping and prostrating himself before the house of God, a*

---

[66]Indeed, the English Standard Version translates 9:5 as follows: *"And at the evening sacrifice I rose from my fasting, with my garment and my cloak torn, and fell upon my knees and spread out my hands to the LORD my God"*

Fasting, Repentance And Revival

very large assembly, men, women, and children, gathered to him from Israel; for the people wept bitterly" (Ezra 10:1). Ezra's time of fasting, humiliation and confession of sin had a powerful effect upon the people of Israel. God used it to ignite a fire of conviction, confession, mourning (as evidenced by their "weeping bitterly") and repentance from sin among the people of God.

3. The people of God fasted in order to mourn their sins. There is also a relationship between fasting and mourning. In the passage from Ezra 10 referred to above the word "mourning" is found in verse 6, *"Then Ezra rose from before the house of God and went into the chamber of Jehohanan the son of Eliashib. Although he went there, he did not eat bread, nor drink water, for he was mourning over the unfaithfulness of the exiles."*

Here we clearly see the relationship between fasting (*"he did not eat . . . nor drink"*) and mourning over sin. Ezra fasted as an expression of mourning over the sin of the people. Ezra didn't simply confess his sin and the sins of the people as some form of "intellectual agreement" with God. It went much deeper. Ezra's heart was broken by the sins which broke the heart of God. It is one thing to intellectually and mentally acknowledge our sin and to confess it. It is quite another when God touches our heart and causes it to break over our sin, just as His heart breaks over our sin, *"Now it came about when I heard these words, I sat down and wept and* **mourned** *for days; and I was fasting and praying before the God of heaven."*

Biblical fasting and mourning over sin isn't self-centered remorse or the hopeless grief of the unbeliever. Instead, biblical fasting and mourning represents our a response to the prompting of the Holy Spirit through which we share in a small measure in God's own grief over our sin. Fasting is a time when we consider and mourn our own sins, failures and shortcomings before God. As John Wesley observed, *"Let every season, either of public or private fasting, be a season of exercising all those holy affections which are implied in a broken and contrite heart. Let it be a season of devout mourning, of godly sorrow for sin. . ."* This is this kind of godly mourning is followed by *"the oil of gladness instead of mourning, the mantle of praise instead of fainting. So they will be called oaks of righteousness, the planting of the Lord, that He may be glorified"* (Isaiah 61:3)

4. The people of God fasted as a profound act of repentance for their sin. Fasting, when combined with humility, confession, and mourning over our sin, represents a profound act of genuine personal repentance. No where is this more clearly seen than in the example of Jonah and the Ninevites. In Jonah 3:5, in response to the preaching of the prophet, *"the people of Nineveh believed in God; and they called a fast and put on sackcloth from the greatest to the least of them."* Their action of fasting represented both an act of faith and an act of profound personal repentance, *"let men call on God earnestly that each may turn from his wicked way and from the violence which is in his hands"* (Jonah 3:8). God graciously accepted the fasting of the Ninevites as an indication of genuine repentance, *"When God saw their deeds, that they turned from their wicked way, then God relented concerning the calamity which He had declared He would bring upon them. And He did not do it"* (Jonah 3:10). Nineveh was spared for another 100 years because the city embraced God's call to repentance.

When the Church lost the consuming fire of God's presence and holiness in its midst, we also lost any sense of our need to repent, along with any sense of how deeply our sin grieves the heart of God. We also lost any need, desire or ability to mourn our sin. In short, we lost our need or reason to

Fasting, Repentance And Revival

humble ourselves through fasting and prayer. Fasting became the pursuit of things - blessings from God - rather than the passionate pursuit of the God Whose presence and holiness are "a consuming fire."

The Inextinguishable Blaze

It is time for the Church to embrace the reality that the pathway to revival leads through the valley of humility, brokenness, confession and repentance. And that path requires a commitment to personal and corporate fasting and prayer, not for things, but for God Himself in sacrificial worship and personal repentance. Are we willing to walk through it? Or are we still looking for ways around it?

Let me leave you with a starting place for your personal devotions. The "Prayer of Confession" on the following page was penned by John Wesley some 250 years ago and has lost none of its significance over the years. Use it as a starting point. Make it your own, and then ask the Holy Spirit to take you deeper into the valley of repentance.

The Inextinguishable Blaze

A Prayer of Confession
by John Wesley

Forgive them all, O Lord:
Our sins of omission and our sins of commission;
The sins of our youth and the sins of our riper years;
The sins of our souls and the sins of our bodies; our secret
and our more open sins;
Our sins of ignorance and surprise, and our more
deliberate and presumptuous sin;
The sins we have done to please ourselves and the sins
we have done to please others;
The sins we know and remember,
and the sins we have forgotten;
The sins we have striven to hide from others,
And the sins by which we have made others offend.
Forgive them, O Lord, forgive them all for His sake,
Who died for our sins and rose for our justification,
And now stands at thy right hand to make intercession for
us, Jesus Christ our Lord.

Chapter 18

The Intimacy of Knowing And Yet Pursuing

*"Indeed, I count everything as loss because of the surpassing worth of **knowing** Christ Jesus my Lord. For his sake I have suffered the loss of all things and count them as rubbish, in order that I may gain Christ and be found in him, not having a righteousness of my own that comes from the law, but that which comes through faith in Christ, the righteousness from God that depends on faith - that I may **know** him and the power of his resurrection, and may share his sufferings, becoming like him in his death, that by any means possible I may attain the resurrection from the dead. Not that I have already obtained this or am already perfect, but I **press on** to make it my own, because Christ Jesus has made me his own. Brothers, I do not consider that I have made it my own. But one thing I do: forgetting what lies behind and straining forward to what lies ahead, I **press on** toward the goal for the prize of the upward call of God in Christ Jesus."* (Philippians 3:8-14)

Place ten believers in a room and ask them to define "intimacy" with God and you will get at least ten different answers. Probably more. And there's the rub. While intimacy with God is neither new nor strange in the life of God's people, few of us can define it with any clarity. Our immediate problem is one of vocabulary. Simply put, intimacy is a term which we have adopted and frequently use, but which is foreign to Scripture. For example, if you search the word "intimate" in the English Standard Version you will find 2 occurrences (Job 19:19 & Proverbs 7:4), neither of which refer to our relationship with God. The word intimacy doesn't occur at all. Upon reflection, what the Church has effectively done is we have adopted a non-biblical term and proceeded to fill it with whatever meaning we want it to have. Intimacy with God has become whatever we want it to be.

The Inextinguishable Blaze

Over the past seventeen chapters we have worked at a basic underlying task: to think right thoughts about God and about ourselves. As we have repeated along the way, the most important thing about any man or woman is what he or she thinks about God, because *"We tend by a secret*

"Wrong thoughts about God and ourselves will produce wrong thoughts about our intimacy with God."

law of the soul to move toward our mental image of God." It was true of the consuming fire of God's holiness; it was true of our response to that fire (repentance); and now it is true of our intimacy with God. Wrong thoughts about God and ourselves will produce wrong thoughts about our intimacy with God.

Earlier in our journey we observed that genuine holiness is about Who you worship, Who you love and Whose image is transforming your life. Holiness, we said, begins with God and ends with us being transformed into His image. Because of Who you love (or fail to love) you can be holy in a dung pile, or unholy in a church meeting.

"Intimacy with God isn't about whether or not we prophesy, cast out demons or perform signs and wonders. Intimacy is about Who we love, Who we worship and Who we pursue."

Genuine holiness begins with the fire of God's Presence and holiness in our hearts and works its way outward through personal confession and repentance into the totality of our lives, not the other way around.

The same is true concerning our intimacy with God. Genuine intimacy with God is about Who you worship, Who you love

The Intimacy Of Knowing And Yet Pursuing

and Whose image is transforming your life. Biblically speaking, intimacy with God isn't about what kind of worship music you enjoy. It isn't about how, when or where you pray, or whether you pray with the tongues of men or of angels. Intimacy with God isn't about your spiritual gift, angelic visitations, or whether you have had a "third heaven" experience. Intimacy with God isn't about giving or receiving prophetic words, casting out demons or performing miracles, a reality that will come as rude awakening to many on the Day of Judgment,

"Not everyone who says to me, 'Lord, Lord,' will enter the kingdom of heaven, but the one who does the will of my Father who is in heaven. On that day many will say to me, 'Lord, Lord, did we not prophesy in your name, and cast out demons in your name, and do many mighty works in your name?' And then will I declare to them, 'I never knew you; depart from me, you workers of lawlessness.'" (Matthew 7:21-23)

Intimacy with God isn't about whether or not we prophesy, cast out demons or perform signs and wonders. Intimacy is about Who we love, Who we worship and Who we pursue.

The Pursuit of The One We Have Found

"Evan Roberts was like a particle of radium in our midst. Its fire was consuming and felt abroad as something which took away sleep, cleared the channels of tears, and sped the golden wheels of prayer throughout the area . . . I did not weep much in the 1859 revival, but I have wept now until my heart is supple. In the midst of the greatest tearfulness I have found the greatest joy. I had felt for a year or two that there was a sighing in the wind, and something whispered that the storm could not be far away. Soon I felt the waters to begin to cascade. Now the bed belongs to the river and Wales

The Inextinguishable Blaze

belongs to Christ." [67]

We all pursue the things which own us, and each of us is owned by the things we pursue. It is one of those unwritten laws of the spiritual life that is as unavoidable as breathing. And for the believer in pursuit of intimacy with God, that intimacy becomes the lifelong and passionate pursuit of the One Who owns us. Genuine intimacy with God, like genuine holiness, begins with God and ends with us being transformed into His image. It begins with the consuming fire of God's Presence and holiness in our hearts and works its way outward through personal confession and repentance into the totality of our lives, including our daily pursuit of"the Inextinguishable Blaze."

The above story from the great Welsh Revival of 1904 is one example of what happens when the God Whose presence and holiness are *"a consuming fire"* rends the heavens, comes down and sets the hearts of men on fire. From that moment

> *"We all pursue the things which own us, and each of us is owned by the things we pursue."*

on they are owned and possessed by the God Whose *"inextinguishable blaze"* burns in their hearts and minds. Their lifelong passion becomes the pursuit of the One they have found and Who now owns them. Just ask the Apostle Paul.

---

[67]Evan Phillips was a child of the 1859 revival in Wales. In 1904 he was a moderator of the Welsh Presbyterian Church and Principal of the "Preparatory School" where Evan Roberts was a first year student. This is his description of Evan Roberts on the eve of the great Welsh Revival of 1904, found in Eifion Evans, **The Welsh Revival Of 1904**, Evangelical Press, 1969, 136 Rosendale Road, London SE 21 or Box 2453, Grand Rapids, Michigan 49501, page 72.

The Intimacy Of Knowing And Yet Pursuing

If anyone in the New Testament understood genuine intimacy with God, it was the Apostle Paul. In His letter to the Philippian believers Paul describes intimacy in terms of his pursuit of God (see Philippians 3:8-14 quoted

"Genuine intimacy with God, like genuine holiness, begins with God and ends with us being transformed into His image."

above). Like Moses standing before Mt. Sinai crying for "more" of the God Whom he has already met (Exodus 33:18), Paul describes his pursuit of intimacy with God in terms of wanting to "know" that which he already "knows," and to obtain the very thing that Jesus had already achieved on his behalf. It is faith combined with fire and passion. In the process, Paul is willing for the consuming fire of God's presence and holiness to consume anything and everything which might hinder that pursuit, even if it means the "loss of all things." This is the language of fire, holiness, daily repentance and undimmed passion. This is the language of a man in pursuit of his "first love." This is the language of a soul in pursuit of the One Who owns him, and who is owned by the One he pursues. It is the language of"the Inextinguishable Blaze." It is the biblical language of genuine intimacy with God.

But is it the language of the Church in the opening decades of the 21st Century? Or is the contemporary Church like the Church of Ephesus in Revelation 2:1-7, a Church that has left the pursuit of its first love and replaced intimacy with activity. Reflecting the zeal of our consumerist culture, contemporary Christians seem to possess more zeal and passion for pursuing sale bargains on Black Friday (the day after Thanksgiving) than for the relentless pursuit of the God Who calls them to *"press on toward the goal for the prize of the upward call of God in Christ Jesus."*

The Inextinguishable Blaze

The Inextinguishable Blaze

It is time for the Church of our generation to recognize and confess that we are, indeed, pursuing the things which own us. Unfortunately, most of those things have little to do with *"the Inextinguishable Blaze"* of God's Presence and holiness. We have substituted the false intimacy of pursuing religious activity for the passionate pursuit of the One Who redeemed us, Who owns us and Who calls us daily to "press on."

It is time for the Church to recover and embrace that intimacy with God which is the passionate pursuit of *"the Inextinguishable Blaze"* of His presence and holiness. As with the Church of Ephesus in Revelation 2, it is time for the Church to once again pursue its "first love." The command of the Risen Christ to the Church of the 21st Century is the same as His command to the Church at Ephesus: *"Remember therefore from where you have fallen, and repent and do the deeds you did at first or else I am coming to you, and will remove your lampstand out of its place—unless you repent."*

Chapter 19

Understanding Biblical Intimacy

"Then he said to Moses, 'Come up to the LORD, you and Aaron, Nadab, and Abihu, and seventy of the elders of Israel, and worship from afar' . . . . Then Moses and Aaron, Nadab, and Abihu, and seventy of the elders of Israel went up, and they saw the God of Israel. There was under his feet as it were a pavement of sapphire stone, like the very heaven for clearness. And he did not lay his hand on the chief men of the people of Israel; they beheld God, and ate and drank."
(Exodus 24:1, 9-11)

Let's begin this Chapter by remembering our journey. Our pursuit of *"the Inextinguishable Blaze"* has taken us through the consuming fire of God's presence and holiness, through repentance as the response of our hearts to the fire of His holiness and, finally, has brought us to the issue of intimacy with God.

Intimacy In The Old Testament.

The scene of the above passage brings us full circle so that we are once again standing at the foot of Mt. Sinai. The people of God in all ages share a common calling. We are called to a relationship of holiness and intimacy with the God Whose presence is *"a consuming fire."* Up 'til now we have examined the fire of God's holiness and the repentance that His fire evokes in the human heart. We now want to consider the biblical foundations for that intimacy which is both the call and the promise of God's people.

Here at the foot of Mt. Sinai the people of Israel met with God and entered into a covenant to be His unique people. In a foretaste of that fellowship in the Kingdom of God which is the expectant hope of every believer, Moses, Aaron, Nadab,

The Inextinguishable Blaze

Abihu and seventy of the elders of Israel were invited to climb Mt. Sinai and meet with God. There upon that mountain *"they saw the God of Israel."* In the very presence of the Holy One of Israel these seventy four men sat (we assume) on a pavement made of clear blue sapphire stone, worshiped "from afar" and - for lack of a better description - ate a picnic lunch. More accurately, they dined in the very Presence of God in a banquet which served as a promise and a foretaste of that great Messianic Banquet which awaits the people of God in the Age to Come (Isaiah 25:6). Welcome to the promise of biblical intimacy.

While the word intimacy doesn't appear in the Old Testament (or the New, for that matter) the concept of a close or intimate relationship with God does appear. Abraham is referred to as a *"friend of God"* (2 Chronicles 20:7; James 2:23). Moses is described as meeting with God and talking with Him *"face to face, as a man speaks to his friend"* (Exodus 33:11).

Throughout the Psalms, David pours out his heart before God in a devotional songbook which portrays a deep, personal and even intimate relationship with God. In the process, David reveals some of the foundations of an intimate relationship with God.

He reveals that it must be pursued, like a deer thirsting for water in a dry land, *"As a deer pants for flowing streams, so pants my soul for you, O God. My soul thirsts for God, for the living God. When shall I come and appear before God?"* (Psalm 42:1-2).

He reveals that it requires personal holiness, "*Who shall ascend the hill of the LORD? And who shall stand in his holy place? He who has clean hands and a pure heart, who does not lift up his soul to what is false and does not swear*

Understanding Biblical Intimacy

deceitfully." (Psalm 24:3-4).

And He reveals that an intimate relationship with God means the privilege of participating in His "secret" or "intimate" counsel, such as friends might share with one another, *"The secret of Jehovah is with those who fear Him; and He will show them His covenant."* (Psalm 25:14)

All of these verses speak of a close, personal and intimate relationship with God that has its foundation in holiness and repentance. Simply put, intimacy with God in the Old Testament is about individuals who by faith have embraced the fire of God's holiness and righteousness. We are told in the New Testament that even Abraham's friendship with God was based on faith and holiness, *"'Abraham believed God, and it was counted to him as righteousness' - and he was called a friend of God."* (James 2:23) Intimacy with God in the Old Testament was not simply about keeping laws and rules. It was about the ceaseless pursuit of the God Whose presence and holiness are *"a consuming fire"* in the midst of His people.

Intimacy In The New Testament.

In the New Testament, a close or personal or intimate relationship between God and His people is described in several different ways, but I want to briefly comment on five of them. Intimacy with God means 1) we know God; 2) we are friends of God; 3) we hear His voice, 4) we have His fellowship; and 5) He is our Father.

Intimacy Means That We Know God. To know God and yet to continue pursuing Him is the heartbeat of New Testament intimacy with God. The New Testament Scriptures are clear that eternal life, life in the Kingdom of God and the Age to Come, cannot be separated from the knowledge of God as

The Inextinguishable Blaze

revealed in His Son, Jesus Christ: *"And this is eternal life, that they know you the only true God, and Jesus Christ whom you have sent."* (John 17:3) But the knowledge of God in Christ by faith is NOT the end of our pursuit of"the Inextinguishable Blaze." It is only the beginning, as we saw in the experience of the Apostle Paul in the book of Philippians. This is the heartbeat of biblical intimacy with God - to know Him and yet to pursue Him in a heart-felt desire for "more." At the same time, it is a pursuit within the Scriptural boundaries of thinking right thoughts about God and ourselves. It is a pursuit founded on the holiness of God, the righteousness of faith in Christ and a genuine repentance from "all things" which might hinder our pursuit for greater intimacy with Him.

Intimacy Means We Are The Friend of God. While the Scriptures do not overly emphasize this aspect of our relationship with God, it is worth reflecting on for a few moments.[68] Since the days of Abraham, the people of God have enjoyed "friendship" with God. The book of James tells us that, *"'Abraham believed God, and it was counted to him as righteousness' - and he was called a friend of God."* (James 2:23) But it has always been a friendship based upon God's holiness and our faith. Biblically speaking, the "friends" of God are those who embrace the fire of His holiness by walking in genuine faith and repentance. We see this in the one passage where Jesus refers to His own disciples as "friends,"

"Greater love has no one than this, that someone lay down

---

[68]The terms "friend" and "friendship" occur some 36 times in the New Testament. Of those occurrences 2 speak of Jesus being the friend of sinners, 1 has to do with Abraham being the friend of God, and 3 are found in John 15 where Jesus calls His disciples friends. The remaining 30 occurrences do not address friendship with God.

Understanding Biblical Intimacy

his life for his friends. You are my friends if you do what I command you. No longer do I call you servants, for the servant does not know what his master is doing; but I have called you friends, for all that I have heard from my Father I have made known to you." (John 15:13-15)

Did you see it? Let me repeat it. *"You are my friends if you do what I command you.*" Friendship with God, to have Jesus call us His "friend" - to be "intimate" with Him - means we embrace the fire of God's holiness and walk in genuine faith, repentance and obedience to His commandments, starting with *"love one another, as I have loved you"* (John 15:12). To be the friend of God is to pursue Him.

Intimacy Means We Hear His Voice. Jesus put it this way, *"My sheep hear my voice, and I know them, and they follow me"* (John 10:27). John Chapter 10 is the "Good Shepherd" chapter of John's Gospel. Jesus' point throughout this chapter is that He is the Good Shepherd, and that His sheep (i.e., believers) hear His voice, while those who are not His sheep (i.e, unbelievers) do not. To know God, and to be known by God, is to hear His voice. To hear God's voice is to pursue Him.

Intimacy Means We Enjoy His Fellowship. One of the more important aspects of our "intimacy"with God is found in the concept of "fellowship," reflected in the following passages:

*"God is faithful, by whom you were called into the **fellowship** of his Son, Jesus Christ our Lord."* (1 Corinthians 1:9)

*"The grace of the Lord Jesus Christ and the love of God and the **fellowship** of the Holy Spirit be with you all."* (2 Corinthians 13:14)

The Inextinguishable Blaze

*"That which we have seen and heard we proclaim also to you, so that you too may have **fellowship** with us; and indeed our **fellowship** is with the Father and with his Son Jesus Christ."* (1 John 1:3)

Our English word "fellowship" translates the Greek word *koinonia*, from the Greek root word *koine*, meaning "common." Fellowship is the holding and sharing of certain things in common. In the life of the Church *koinonia* represents a mutual sharing of our lives together. In Revelation 1:9 the Apostle John uses a derivative of *koinonia* (*sugkoinonos*) as he explains to His readers that believers share a common *"tribulation and kingdom and perseverance which are in Jesus."* Certain things are common to the Christian experience, and fellowship - both with God and with one another - is one of them.

Our fellowship impacts us in two primary ways. Through the redeeming work of Jesus on the cross we have been called into fellowship with God (Father, Son and Holy Spirit). This is New Testament intimacy with God. This "intimate fellowship" with God occurs on terms which are clear and unequivocal: the embracing of His holiness and repentance from sin. To claim fellowship or intimacy with God on any other terms apart from these is a lie and a deception. How do we know? Because Scripture clearly tells us, *"If we say we have fellowship with Him while we walk in darkness, we lie and do not practice the truth."* (1 John 1:6) This truth is restated by Peter:

*"His divine power has granted to us all things that pertain to life and godliness, through the knowledge of him who called us to his own glory and excellence, by which he has granted to us his precious and very great promises, so that through them you may become **partakers** of the divine nature, having escaped from the corruption that is in the world because of*

Understanding Biblical Intimacy

sinful desire." (2 Peter 1:3-4)

According to Peter, we now "share" or "partake" (Greek: *koinonos*) in God's nature, a nature which by definition is "holy, holy, holy." By faith in Christ and by the indwelling of the Holy Spirit, we now share the consuming fire of God's holiness. And fire takes no prisoners. It either burns us beyond recognition, or it consumes us until we become carriers of the fire. We pursue the fire which consumes us, and we are consumed by the fire we pursue.

The second impact of "intimate fellowship" is to lay a foundation for a renewed fellowship with other believers: *"But if we walk in the light, as he is in the light, we have fellowship with one another, and the blood of Jesus his Son cleanses us from all sin."* (1 John 1:7) As a community of believers we share a common "fire" of holiness and repentance. That same divine fire of holiness and repentance which gives us intimate fellowship with God also gives us genuine fellowship (or "intimacy") with one another in that community of believers we call "the Church."

> *"We pursue the fire which consumes us, and we are consumed by the fire we pursue."*

In the New Testament, this fellowship, this genuine *koinonia*, expressed itself in home-based Churches where believers shared their lives with one another. They shared meals together in one another's homes. They prayed together, endured persecution together, worshiped together and, at times, they died together. They preferred one another's company above all others and gave sacrificially to meet each other's needs. They passionately pursued the fire which consumed them and were consumed by the fire they passionately pursued. Whenever possible, they gathered

The Inextinguishable Blaze

together in one another's homes to worship the One they passionately pursued, and to pursue together the One they passionately loved. Through it all they found "intimate fellowship" with God and with one another.

Intimacy Means God Is Our Father. The idea of God as "father" is as old as the Scriptures. The Old Testament spoke of God as *"Father of the fatherless and protector of widows is God in his holy habitation."* (Psalm 68:5). The Psalmist addressed God as *"my Father, my God, and the Rock of my salvation."*(Psalms 89:26. See also Isaiah 9:6; 63:16; 64:8; Jeremiah 31:9). But it is in the New Testament that the fatherhood of God is further developed to reflect two events: *"the incarnation"* and *"the adoption."* The Fatherhood of God becomes prominent in the New Testament because of the incarnation of the second Person of the Trinity - Jesus, the Son of God. As a result the New Testament frequently refers to God as *"the God and Father of our Lord Jesus Christ"* (see Romans 15:6; 2 Corinthians 1:3, 11:31; Ephesians 1:3; 1 Peter 1:3). Because of the incarnation, the Fatherhood of God took on a prominence not known in the Old Testament.

> *"Because of the incarnation, the Fatherhood of God took on a prominence not known in the Old Testament."*

But the Fatherhood of God comes to prominence in the New Testament for another reason: the "adoption" of believers as "sons of God." The Apostle Paul writes about this in his letter to the Church in Rome, *"For you did not receive the spirit of slavery to fall back into fear, but you have received the Spirit of adoption as sons, by whom we cry, 'Abba! Father!'"* (Romans 8:15) Through his sacrificial and atoning death on

Understanding Biblical Intimacy

the cross, Jesus paid the price to redeem us from the slave market of sin (Paul talks about this at length in Romans Chapter 6). We have now been *"bought with a price"* (1 Corinthians 7:23) and the price of our freedom

"Biblical intimacy with God means that we now have the right to address God as our Father."

from slavery has been paid. If God's redemptive plan had ended there - with our release from slavery - it would have been more than we deserved. We would be "freedmen." But there is more. Not only did Jesus pay the price of our redemption (or "manumission") from slavery to sin and set us free, but God the Father has adopted us into His family as "sons" (see Romans 8:15 & 23; Romans 9:4; Galatians 4:5; Ephesians 1:5). Biblical intimacy with God means that we now have the right to address God as our Father.

Fatherhood, Majesty And Intimacy

"Out of the north comes golden splendor; God is clothed with awesome majesty." (Job 37:22)

"The LORD reigns; he is robed in majesty." (Psalms 93:1)

"To the only God, our Savior, through Jesus Christ our Lord, be glory, majesty, dominion, and authority, before all time and now and forever. Amen." (Jude 1:25)

I was a young, precocious campus Christian radical at the University of North Carolina (Chapel Hill) when I attended a conference sponsored by Campus Crusade for Christ. At that Conference Josh McDowell gave a series of lectures on the attributes of God. He entitled the series *"He May Be Your*

The Inextinguishable Blaze

Father, But He's Not Your Old Man.[69] That series of lectures had a profound impact on me as a young believer, and what stuck with me all these years was the title. It touched a chord in my own heart about how we as the Church view our relationship with God.

There has always been a certain "majesty" in the Church's relationship with God, at least until lately. One of the unfortunate consequences of thinking wrong thoughts about God in our generation has been a profound loss of any sense of the majesty of God. It has become one of our common modern idolatries to think too little of God. This includes the truth about the Fatherhood of God. Contemporary Christians seem to think that they are the first generation of believers to discover that God is their Father. We are not, of course. But we are the first generation to turn the Fatherhood of God into a full-blown personal therapy. The Holy One of Israel, the God Who reigns on high and is clothed in splendor and majesty has been reduced to little more than a memory and a figure head, replaced by a more modern and therapeutic idolatry called "pappa" or "daddy." I occasionally get e-mails from people who think it is biblical and more spiritual to refer to God as "daddy" or "pappa." It isn't. But it is more therapeutic. It makes them feel better.

This is usually defended by a reference to Romans 8:15 where Paul refers to God as "Abba, Father." The term "Abba," they argue means "daddy." This is incorrect. The term "Abba" is the Greek rendering of the Aramaic word for "Father," used by both children and adults to address their "father." The commentary on Matthew 6:9 in the *English*

---

[69]The internet is becoming "the world's archive." You can find notes from this series posted online on Josh's ministry website at www.josh.org.

Understanding Biblical Intimacy

Standard Study Bible captures the issue as follows: *"It was the word used by Jewish children for their earthly fathers. However, since the term in both Aramaic and Greek was also used by adults to address their fathers, the claim that "Abba" meant "Daddy" is misleading and runs the risk of irreverence."* The rendering of "daddy" or "pappa" misrepresents the meaning of Abba by creating a diminutive term which shrinks God down to our level and diminishes His majesty.

Personally, I am all in favor of feeling better, but not at the expense of God's Majesty. And I have no interest in quenching anyone's intimacy with the God Who has redeemed them from slavery and adopted them into His family. But intimacy must be on God's terms, not ours, and it begins by thinking right thoughts about Who God is and who we are in relation to Him. *He may be your Father, but He's not your dad.*

The Inextinguishable Blaze

It is time for the Church of our generation to recover its heritage of genuine intimacy with the God Whose presence and holiness are *"a consuming fire,"* but Whose heart is that of a Father toward the "son" (or "daughter") he has redeemed from slavery and sin. The world of our generation is perishing because it has yet to see the fire and the power of a genuinely intimate Church. Are you prepared to show it to them?

The Inextinguishable Blaze

Chapter 20

Reflections On Job, Repentance and Intimacy

"Then Job answered the Lord, and said, 'I know that Thou canst do all things, And that no purpose of Thine can be thwarted. 'Who is this that hides counsel without knowledge?' Therefore I have declared that which I did not understand, things too wonderful for me, which I did not know. 'Hear, now, and I will speak; I will ask Thee, and do Thou instruct me.' I have heard of Thee by the hearing of the ear; But now my eye sees Thee; therefore I abhor myself, and I repent in dust and ashes."

I'll go out on a limb here, but I think I am safe in saying that few Christians have ever turned to the Book of Job as a guide to greater intimacy with God. In fact, my guess from personal experience is that most Christians go through their lives hoping to avoid either reading or understanding the book of Job, much less turning to it for advice on their relationship with God. And I would go on to venture that there's scarcely a believer among us whose prayer list includes, *"Lord, make me like Job."* But through his ordeal Job came to a profound understanding of God's holiness, sovereignty and majesty, as well as to a depth of repentance and renewed faith that we could all learn from. So, let's join Job on his journey and take good notes.

Setting The Stage For A Morality Play

Let's do a quick overview. The Book of Job is a "morality play" in six parts: A Prologue, four Acts and an Epilogue. Job is a human actor in a divine drama of which he is unaware. The notion of believers as actors in a cosmic drama is suggested in 1 Corinthians Chapter 4 where Paul refers to apostles as "spectacles" to the world. The Greek word there is *theatron* from which we get our English word *"theater."* Get

The Inextinguishable Blaze

the idea?

In the Prologue (Job Chapters 1-2) we see the stage being set with the major players. In the Prologue we are specifically told (twice, 1:22 & 2:10) that Job was a righteous man who had not sinned. If you miss this point, the next 34 chapters can get VERY confusing as Job's religious paradigm regarding sin, righteousness, suffering and God's dealings with people gets seriously challenged. Job is getting divinely set up for a radical paradigm shift. Job gets some help with his paradigm shift from three friends and a stranger. These four people combine to communicate one message: *"You've sinned, and that's why God has allowed this trial. God doesn't do this to people who haven't sinned."* Through four long and sometimes tedious Acts, these four "counselors" repeat their arguments and thereby reveal their religious boxes. And poor Job simply doesn't fit into any of their pre-packaged religious boxes.

Bildad the Shuhite is the "traditionalist," always appealing to what the fathers have said about the situation because there was nothing new to be learned. He is a traditionalist and he looks back in history to find what others have already said. He has a high regard for truth and sees it as inherited, not to be messed with, something wrestled over by the elders, handed down to those eager for wisdom, and eventually passed on to the next generation.[70]

Zophar is the "rationalist" *who appeals to rational wisdom and hints that Job is witless or stupid. He also gives a*

---

[70]My thanks to Andrew Jones, otherwise known on the web as "TallSkinnyKiwi" (http://tallskinnykiwi.typepad.com/) for his excellent article "The Skinny on Post Modernity - Part 1" for some excellent insights into Job. His thoughts appear in italics.

formula that if Job does certain things, then a favorable outcome will result. This makes Zophar the "apologist" of the group, always ready with a tightly crafted argument which always yields the righ" conclusion. But I would also suggest that this makes Zophar an unwitting model for what I call Christian magicians, believers who are looking for magic formulas which they can use to manipulate God: *"If you do A, B and C, God will always do D."* Such people are the "Harry Potters" of the church who regard the things of God as formulas to be followed or spells to be cast in order to get the desired result. Those same people will turn holiness, repentance and intimacy into a set of rules for behavior (or they'll just insist that you keep the Old Testament laws).

Eliphaz is the "mystic" in the bunch whose "authority" is to appeal to his experiences to prove his point. *He had a dream and his hair stood on end. A spirit appeared. This was proof enough. He sees God as one who "performs wonders that cannot be fathomed."*

Then there's Elihu, the "stranger" who turns out to be the "theologian" of the group. You know the type. The young turk fresh out of seminary whose passion exceeds his wisdom and whose response is something like, *"How dare you question God. What you need is a good systematic theology to straighten out your squishy belief system."*

These four "counselors" combined together to present Job with explanations which didn't explain and left Job with a "pain in the mind" (to loosely quote Leslie Newbigin) which would not go away. The answers given by his friends were the standard answers of the prevailing religious paradigm as they understood it. Andrew Jones observes, *"A funny thing about the Book of Job is that each guy, with such radically differing thought processes, comes to the same conclusion - Job has sinned and is therefore suffering. Even funnier is*

217

The Inextinguishable Blaze

the fact that all three men are wrong. The truth in this case is something more complicated and mysterious. But watching them think is worth the exercise since they represent how people think in general." Very true.

My perspective is that Job's counselors were all "right" according to the prevailing religious paradigm of the day, a paradigm which Job probably shared up until this fateful series of events. But none of their right answers were valid in Job's situation (hence, their frustration and Job's despair). They were offering "boxed" answers to an "outside the box" situation. Like many believers today, they were giving Job the right answers to the wrong question. They wanted intimacy with God, but only on terms of their own understanding, which was now being seriously challenged.

Job was on a spiritual journey that no one seemed to understand or appreciate, including Job, his wife, his friends and a significant number of readers and commentators in the 3500 years since then! When faced with a spiritually unknown situation our first and most consistent tendency is to fall back into "truisms" - answers that are "usually true" and have served us in the past. But "boxed answers" and our tendencies to use them when in doubt can quickly turn knowledge into the enemy of learning. It wasn't until God made a personal appearance, thirty eight chapters into this play, and revealed Himself both to Job and his inquisitors, that we begin to understand the truth of what is taking place. God then spends four chapters revealing His greatness and exposing Job's insignificance: *"I'm God. I'm Holy. You're not. Get used to it."* How profound is this message? Well, after

"But 'boxed answers' and our tendencies to use them when in doubt can quickly turn knowledge into the enemy of learning."

Reflections On Job, Repentance And Intimacy

3500 years, we still haven't quite gotten used to it.

The Epilogue (And Punch Line)

Then Job answered the Lord, and said, "I know that Thou canst do all things, And that no purpose of Thine can be thwarted. 'Who is this that hides counsel without knowledge?' Therefore I have declared that which I did not understand, things too wonderful for me, which I did not know. 'Hear, now, and I will speak; I will ask Thee, and do Thou instruct me.' I have heard of Thee by the hearing of the ear; But now my eye sees Thee; therefore I retract, and I repent in dust and ashes."

The five poetical books of the Old Testament - including the book of Job - are all about intimacy with God, but it is intimacy on His terms, not ours. The Book of Job teaches us both the holiness and the sovereignty of God over His created order and over human suffering. It also reminds us of God's transcendent holiness as He stands apart from His creation while ruling it and bending it to His will. This understanding of the sovereignty and the transcendent holiness of God should lead us to the fear of God and to worship (Psalms). Worship and fear give way to wisdom (Proverbs). Wisdom, born of worship and the fear of God, gives us the understanding and stability we need to overcome the seeming vanity of life (Ecclesiastes) while encouraging us to pursue God as one pursues the lover of our soul (Song of Songs).

In the Epilogue of the play, Job must come to terms with what has now become nothing less than a personal confrontation with the holiness and sovereignty of God. It is a rude but necessary awakening and we get to watch it unfold as Job quotes God's own words back to Him, *'Who is this that hides counsel without knowledge?'* In the process

The Inextinguishable Blaze

Job must confront his own idolatry - his own wrong thinking about God. For example, Job confesses that he has *"declared that which I did not understand."* The sense of the Hebrew here is that Job had *"boldly proclaimed"* things about God which were not true and regarding which he really knew nothing at all. That's what happens when you repeat the idolatries and opinions of others. In a truly humbling moment, Job quotes God's own words back to Him, *"'Hear, now, and I will speak; I will ask Thee, and do Thou instruct me.'"* (Compare Job 40:7 & 42:4). Earlier, God had invited Job to teach Him. Now, at last, Job understands who is the teacher and who is the student. That's a humbling moment for the theological "know-it-alls" among us (ahem!). The "punch line" for the Epilogue occurs in verses 5-6:

"I have heard of Thee by the hearing of the ear; But now my eye sees Thee; therefore I retract, and I repent in dust and ashes."

This *"moment of clarity"* contained three insights which affect us as much as they affect Job. **First**, like Isaiah in the Temple, Job came to a new understanding of Who God is. In a painful moment of divine confrontation Job moved from possessing a second-hand knowledge of God passed down from others (*"by the hearing of the ear"*) to a first-hand knowledge of God that was personal, experiential and, yes, even intimate.

Second, Job had one of those rare moments of personal introspection when - standing in the presence of this holy and transcendent God - he realized how wrong he had been about God. Like Isaiah in the Temple crying out *"Woe is me, for I am ruined!"* the result for Job was a moment of genuine grief and personal self-loathing as he was forced to confront the idolatries of his own heart. The NASB rendering of "retract" represents more modern psychology than Hebrew nuance. The older KJV is closer to the sense of the Hebrew: *"I abhor myself."*[71] If you have never had one of those moments alone with God when you weep the tears of the broken hearted over of how wrong you have been about God - and how you have shared your ignorance and your idolatries with others - then it may be your time. It will be a critical moment on your journey into holiness, repentance and greater spiritual intimacy with God. Genuine intimacy with God must be built upon the truth of Who God is, not upon our idolatries and misconceptions of Who He is. As Job discovered, *"He may be your Father, but He's not your dad."*

The **third** thing that happened to Job came to him as the result of the other two. Job experienced a genuine encounter with God, resulting in a genuine change of heart, mind and attitude toward God. In other words, Job experienced genuine personal repentance. Back in Chapter 14 we learned about the two primary Hebrew words for "repent" in the Old Testament. The first and most common is "*shuwb*" which simply means "to turn," resulting in a change of behavior or direction. The second word is "*nacham*" which means *"to have a change of heart, attitude, mind or purpose."* This second word is the one that appears here in Job 42:6. As a result of his profound encounter with God's transcendent holiness and sovereignty, Job experienced a change of heart and mind about God and His dealings in his own life, resulting in greater personal intimacy with God.

O, Lord, Make Me Like Job

We have now come full circle. God's morality play starring God, Satan, Job, his family and a supporting cast of

---

[71]The English Standard Version gets closer, rendering this verse as *"therefore I despise myself, and repent in dust and ashes."*

The Inextinguishable Blaze

"counselors" is now over. As we, the Audience, file out of the theater the question hanging in the air for us to take home and ponder is, *"What did we learn about Who God is and our relationship with Him?"* Allow me to suggest several possible lessons.

Perhaps we found ourselves identifying with one of the characters and their broken religious paradigm. After all, one of the purposes of any good morality play is to hold a mirror up to the audience and to ask if they see themselves reflected there. Job's counselors had been wrong about God and His dealings with Job, *"My anger burns against you and against your two friends, for you have not spoken of me what is right, as my servant Job has."* (Job 42:7) How about you? Have you been wrong, too, about God's holiness, majesty and sovereignty and about your own need for repentance?

Perhaps we learned something regarding our own idolatries and misconceptions about God and how they affect our intimacy with Him. Both Job and his counselors were guilty of thinking wrong thoughts about God and how He worked. When finally confronted by God, Job was willing to humble himself and repent. What about us? Are we willing to confess our personal idolatries and repent?

Perhaps we learned that personal repentance and intimacy with God are related, even inseparable. In the process, perhaps we learned that without genuine humility and repentance there can be no genuine intimacy with God. For some of us, that alone is a life changing revelation.

Perhaps we learned that without a genuine encounter with God's transcendent holiness, we all tend to avoid repentance in favor of clinging to our idolatries.

Reflections On Job, Repentance And Intimacy

Perhaps we learned that genuine intimacy with God is somehow dependent upon our willingness to humble ourselves, repent and learn new things about the God Whom we claim to know and Whom we claim to worship in Spirit and in Truth.

Perhaps . . .

Just as the fear of God is the beginning of wisdom, so too, holiness and repentance are the beginning of genuine intimacy. But the road into genuine intimacy with God will look different for each person, because God deals with each of us as individuals. There are no formulas or programs for this. Just as holiness is a person and a relationship, so too, intimacy is personal and relational. There is no formula or program for achieving it.

But as we are traveling on this road to holiness, repentance and intimacy, you and I will occasionally meet up with other people who are on this journey - children of the burning heart in pursuit of *"the Inextinguishable Blaze"* which now possesses them. I have two sure-fire ways of knowing

> *"Just as the fear of God is the beginning of wisdom, so too, holiness and repentance are the beginning of genuine intimacy."*

when I have encountered another fellow traveler on this journey. *First,* when they think no one is watching you will see them walk with a limp. Like Job, Jacob, Paul and countless saints who have walked this path, they carry a daily reminder of that divine encounter which transformed their spiritual lives and left them ablaze with holy fire. And *second*, when they think no one is listening you will occasionally hear them whisper a quiet prayer: *"Father,*

The Inextinguishable Blaze

forgive me. I had heard of Thee by the hearing of the ear; But now my eye sees Thee; therefore I abhor myself, and I repent in dust and ashes."

Welcome to this amazing journey into holiness, repentance and intimacy with God. And so long as we're traveling together . . . feel free to limp.

Chapter 21

If Only He Could Trust Us

"The evening service was terrible. So near was the revivalist to his God, that his face shone like that of an angel, so that none could gaze steadfastly at him. Many of the hearers swooned. On the way home I dared not break the silence for miles. Towards midnight I ventured to say, 'Didn't we have blessed meetings, Mr. Morgan?' 'Yes,' he replied; and after a pause, added, 'The Lord would give us great things, if He could only trust us'. 'What do you mean?' I asked. 'If He could trust us not to steal the glory for ourselves.' Then the midnight air rang with his cry, at the top of his voice, 'Not unto us, O Lord, not unto us, but unto Thy name give glory'."[72]

David Morgan, the subject of the above story from the Welsh Revival of 1859, was a man possessed by *"the Inextinguishable Blaze"* of God's presence and transcendent holiness; a man in pursuit of the One Who owned him. Morgan was a pastor in the Calvinistic Methodist Church of Wales when the Revival of 1859 began to take hold. Up until that time his ministry had been faithful, but not extra-ordinary. Then it happened. It happened in the early days of the revival. According to his son and biographer, Morgan went to bed one evening as ususal. When he awoke the next morning he was keenly aware that something had changed. Like Moses after his encounter with God on Mt. Sinai, Morgan's life now radiated a Presence and a Power he had not previously known. It affected him in several ways. *"I was aware that I could remember everything I had ever learned of a religious nature,"* he later commented. In addition to this

---

[72]Eifion Evans, *Revival Comes to Wales: The story of the 1859 Revival in Wales* (Christian Literature Crusade; 3rd edition 1979).

The Inextinguishable Blaze

new "total recall," Morgan also discovered that he could meet large numbers of people and later recall the names of every one of them in the order he had met them. But perhaps the greatest change was in his preaching. Prior to that night his preaching had been faithful. Now, it became truly powerful to the conversion of souls. For the next two years David Morgan, "the evangelist" (as he came to be known), crisscrossed Wales preaching with this new-found power. It is estimated that upwards of 100,000 souls came to new faith in Christ as Savior as a result, and David Morgan, "the evangelist," became a household name in Wales. Welcome to the outworking of *"the Inextinguishable Blaze"* in the lives of those who pursue Him, and who, in the midst of their pursuit, are found by Him.

Can He Trust Us?

"For the eyes of the LORD run to and fro throughout the whole earth, to give strong support to those whose heart is blameless toward him." (2 Chronicles 16:9)

These words of Hanani the Seer to King Asa are as relevant to us today as they were to the wayward King. They accurately describe the twin themes of this book, which has now reached its closing moments. Our first and dominant theme has involved the pressing need of the Church to think right thoughts about God and ourselves by seeking Him in holiness and fear, genuine personal repentance and renewed intimacy. This theme describes what it means to be "children of the burning heart," believers engaged in the active, daily and life-long pursuit of the God Whose Presence and holiness are "a consuming fire" in the midst of His people.

The above verse also describes our second theme, namely, that of spiritual awakening and revival. In every generation of

If Only He Could Trust Us

believers God searches for those who are willing to seek Him on His terms. But the history of God's people, both in Scripture as well as in the Church, tells us that this is uniquely true prior to and during seasons of spiritual awakening. Prior to seasons of spiritual awakening God looks for "forerunners" who are willing to surrender their lives unreservedly to *"the inextinguishable blaze,"* to weep, fast and pray for their generation and to wrestle with God while crying out, *"Great God, give me Scotland, or I shall die."*[73]

During seasons of spiritual awakening and outpouring God looks for men (and women) like David Morgan who are willing to be greatly used of God, people whom He can trust not to "steal" His glory for themselves. I have often mused if, perhaps, one of the reasons revival and spiritual awakening tarry in our generation is because God sees far too many leaders in the Church who would quickly co-opt God's glorious dealings among His people to launch a fund raising campaign to support their worldwide television ministry, announce a building program or market a book/sermon/DVD package. In short, there are just too many leaders who simply cannot be trusted not to compete with God for that glory which is His alone.

Can you and I be trusted not to steal God's glory for ourselves and our ministries?

A Bride Holy And Blameless

." . . . *that He might present to Himself the church in all her*

---

[73]The famous prayer of John Knox, founder of the Church of Scotland, as recorded by Robert Fleming, **Fulfilling Of The Scripture** (Stephen Young, 1801 Edition) p. 423. Available online as a Google PDF scanned book.

The Inextinguishable Blaze

glory, having no spot or wrinkle or any such thing; but that she should be holy and blameless." (Ephesians 5:27)

Over the years I have heard numerous speakers Christians declare that before Jesus returns He wants a bride that is holy and blameless, without any spot, wrinkle or blemish. What is nearly always left out of the declaration is any serious reflection on how God intends to bring this about. You and I are left with the impression that God is going to wave His magic miracle wand over the Church and we will all wake up one day (much to our pleasant surprise) holy and blameless.

I, too, believe that God wants to produce a bride *"having no spot or wrinkle or any such thing."* But I also believe that God has a plan for bringing this about, one which doesn't involve magic wands. I believe God intends to bring about a season of spiritual awakening and revival the likes of which the Church in America and the West has not seen in well over 100 years. As part of this season of spiritual awakening and revival He intends to give His Church a genuine "Isaiah 6" experience of His holiness (and fear), to return genuine personal repentance over sin to His Church, and to bring His Church into a renewed intimacy with Himself. In short, I believe God intends to once again set the Church of this generation on fire with *"the Inextinguishable Blaze"* of His presence and holiness. This has been both the heritage and the hope of those seasons of profound spiritual awakening and divine visitation that we call "revival."

Where Do We Go From Here?

We've come to the end of our journey into the consuming fire of God's presence and holiness, the repentance it elicits from the human heart and the pursuit of intimacy it ignites like an inextinguishable blaze. But in this journey, any ending is

If Only He Could Trust Us

merely a pause before we renew our pursuit of the One Whose fire has captivated our hearts and Who now owns us.

If you were looking for a *"40 Days of Holiness, Repentance and Intimacy"* program at this point, you're about to be sorely disappointed. Moses didn't have one, neither did Isaiah. There is no New Testament "plan" for holiness, repentance and intimacy (although I have no doubt that someone will try to create one - if someone hasn't already done so). The biblical reality is that God in the beauty of His holiness is a Person to be sought, not a program to be launched. The consuming fire of His holiness is a relationship to be pursued, not a formula to be implemented. He desires your heart, your faith and your obedience. He desires your life-long pursuit of *"the Inextinguishable Blaze"* of His Presence and holiness, not your attendance at a class on how to be more "holy." The only question remaining is this: Are you prepared to seek Him in holiness and fear, in genuine personal repentance and in genuine intimacy with Him. The fate of a perishing world may well depend upon your answer.

> *Jesus, confirm my heart's desire*
> *To work, and speak, and think for thee;*
> *Still let me guard the holy fire,*
> *And still stir up thy gift in me;*
> *Ready for all thy perfect will,*
> *My acts of faith and love repeat,*
> *Till death thy endless mercies seal,*
> *And make the sacrifice complete.*

www.ingramcontent.com/pod-product-compliance
Lightning Source LLC
Chambersburg PA
CBHW071422090426
42737CB00011B/1539